COM
ATT

COMMAND ATTENTION

Promoting Your Organization
The Marine Corps Way

Col. Keith Oliver, USMC (Ret.)

Foreword by Joe Galloway
Famed war correspondent and coauthor of
We Were Soldiers Once . . . and Young

NAVAL INSTITUTE PRESS
Annapolis, Maryland

Naval Institute Press
291 Wood Road
Annapolis, MD 21402

Library of Congress Cataloging-in-Publication Data
Oliver, Keith.
 Promoting your organization the Marine Corps way / Keith Oliver.
    p. cm.
 Includes bibliographical references and index.
 ISBN 978-1-59114-645-2 (alk. paper)
 1. United States. Marine Corps—Public relations—Handbooks, manuals,
etc. 2. Public relations—Handbooks, manuals, etc. I. Title.
 VE23.O45 2009
 659.2—dc22

                            2009025844

Printed in the United States of America on acid-free paper

14 13 12 11 10 09   9 8 7 6 5 4 3 2
First printing

Book design and composition: David Alcorn, Alcorn Publication Design

For Ceresse
1954–2007
the best girl a Marine ever had

PROVERBS 31:10–31

CONTENTS

FOREWORD

Who knew the Marines needed help with their public relations when they've done it so beautifully for a couple of centuries or so?

In fact, I always thought that the Marines wrote the book when it comes to the arcane art of military public relations. But it turns out that they don't have such a book, so my old friend Col. Keith Oliver, USMC (Ret.), has written one for them and anyone else interested in doing PR right.

Command Attention: Promoting Your Organization the Marine Corps Way is that book.

Of course, it is a great help if the organization you want to promote is the U.S. Marine Corps, the Leathernecks, the Gyrenes, who have written their history on a hundred beaches in a score of our nation's wars.

The Marines have always been certain that they are the best—that they have the best fighting men and women, the best uniform, the best attitude, the best and meanest drill instructors. The difficult they do right away. The impossible takes a bit longer.

When I first turned up in South Vietnam in the spring of 1965 the only combat units who had arrived by then were Marines, and I was dispatched to Danang to report on them.

At that point the Marines had already commandeered a former French merchant marine brothel on the banks of the Danang River and turned it into the Marine Press Center, where a small but growing corps of war correspondents lived, worked, and ate with Marines—when we weren't in the field covering the Marines.

There we met and became good friends with old gunny sergeants who had first fought at the Chosin Reservoir in

Korea and gray-haired colonels and generals who had fought at Guadalcanal and Iwo Jima and Okinawa. In the field we marched with Marine battalions commanded by young officers like Lt. Col. P. X. Kelly.

We came and went; we marched with other great outfits and commanders in the Army's 1st Cavalry Division (Airmobile) and the 82nd Airborne and the Big Red One during multiple tours in Vietnam. But there was always a warm spot in our hearts for the Marines, for the simple genius of their open hands and open hearts.

Alone among America's military services, the Marines made public relations and military-media relations look easy. They always welcomed the reporters, photographers, and television cameras, eager to give them free and easy access to the young Marines, who are the Corps' proudest and most important product.

I tagged along with Americans at war for over four decades. My last outing with the Marines was in 2006 in Fallujah and Al Asad in Iraq, and, by then, even the gray-haired colonels and generals looked young to me. Their proudest product is still their young Marines.

Keith Oliver has written a lively, literate, useful handbook on how the Marines do public relations, media relations, and community relations for new arrivals in the Corps, for junior officers assigned public affairs as one of many "other duties" on their plate, and for new commanders who may need a reminder of just how important PR is to their success.

He covers all the bases, sprinkles each chapter with useful and entertaining anecdotes and pithy quotes, and lays it all out so it is easily accessible and understandable.

Oliver is a past master at the art of PR, handling tough public affairs assignments at U.S. Central Command forward headquarters in Qatar in the 2003 invasion of Iraq, at Camp Lejeune, in Beirut and Mogadishu, and at Marine Corps Headquarters in Washington, D.C.

All of which is by way of saying that he knows whereof he speaks, and it just doesn't get much better than it does in these pages.

If the organization you are promoting is not the U.S. Marine Corps, you have your job cut out for you, and this book will make it easier.

Joseph L. Galloway
Nationally syndicated military columnist
War correspondent Vietnam, Persian Gulf War,
   Haiti, and Iraq
Coauthor of *We Were Soldiers Once . . . and Young*
We Are Soldiers Still
Triumph Without Victory

ACKNOWLEDGMENTS

Lotsa Help Along the Way

> Moreover, when God gives any man wealth and pos-
> sessions, and enables him to enjoy them, to accept his
> lot and be happy in his work—this is a gift of God.
> He seldom reflects on the days of his life, because
> God keeps him occupied with gladness of heart.
>
> ECCLESIASTES 5:19–20

Tom Cutler is an interesting and colorful figure at the U.S.
Naval Academy, humming away at a manuscript or article from his perch at Beach Hall overlooking the ceme-
tery or walking in "The Yard" with Dutton, his little Westie, in
tow. A former enlisted sailor, Tom authored *A Sailor's History
of the U.S. Navy* (in addition to numerous other works), and
in the mid-1980s, we were faculty colleagues in the Division
of English and History at Sampson Hall. He's now in his second decade with the Naval Institute Press, publishers of this
book.

It was Tom's telephone call in 2006 that planted the seed
for *Command Attention*; I shall always be grateful for his initiative that day—and for his encouragement since.

The Naval Institute, of course, is a team—and while Tom
was the impetus, there are many members of Team USNI,
including alumni, whom I sincerely thank: Jim Barber, Jim
Caiella, Susan Corrado, Judy Heise, Chas Henry, Laura
Johnston, Gary Kessler, Paul Merzlak, John Miller, Fred
Rainbow, Fred Shultz, Paul Stillwell, Bob Timberg, and Tom
Wilkerson.

Several dear friends and relatives read various drafts and
chapters of *Command Attention*, chief among them Dan and

Darlene Heath; Jim and Dawn Diehl; Lt. Col. Riccoh Player, and Maj. "Buzzard" Miller.

Meaningful encouragement came from many quarters, including that from my fantastic daughter, Roxanne (a.k.a. The "Z" Girl); neighbors Wayne and Cynthia Bixby and Hank and Donna Sengelaub; and my beloved brother, Steve Oliver.

A prolific reader (and sage adviser) from the days of our storied youth, Steve is three years my junior, but I publicly declared him my "big brother" at my promotion-to-colonel ceremony in 2001. Everybody needs a big brother; I have the best.

Also, friends Debbie Mallow, Frank Urben, Jackie Ostrom, Dawn Martini, Joe Galloway, Sandi McKenna, Dave Danelo, and my former pastor, Chris Peeler.

Silent (and unknowing) partners were authors of three nightstand books I finished during the final couple months of writing: D. Michael Abrashoff (*It's Your Ship*), Torie Clarke (*Lipstick on a Pig*), and Jim Webb (*A Time to Fight*).

Besides their great insights that have helped me in my teaching, leading, and citizenry, all three writers showed me that *Command Attention* need not be some sort of dry, heavily footnoted textbook. Instead, I have shared my own experiences herein, and I leave it to you, gentle reader, to judge whether or not the tale has been worth the telling.

For basic motivation, fellow Marine Steven Pressfield's *The War of Art* (New York: Warner Books, 2002) is a nice little shot of espresso for any aspiring writer, and it certainly was for this one. See, especially, his "What a Writer's Day Feels Like," on pages 65–67.

So to these and others who contributed to the successful launch of this boat, thank you. I also beg your forgiveness for the inevitable, inadvertent omissions!

For the *content* and for allowing me to pursue my life's work, it's another group of folks I gratefully acknowledge.

Jim and Marion Oliver raised six children on a shoestring budget, but in a home where we watched the news every night, listened to WLCO-AM at breakfast every morning, and subscribed to the weekly *Lake Region News*, the (Leesburg) *Daily Commercial,* and the "big city" *Orlando Sentinel.*

Even more impressive were the magazines on the coffee table that went beyond *Newsweek* and *Good Housekeeping* to include those pertaining to Scouting, hospital administration, and civic and veterans organizations. We did not watch a whole lot of television after supper because we were always going to meetings, playing sports, or participating in service projects. Some people call that "giving back." Our role model parents showed us—never told us—that that's what we're *supposed* to do.

My fellow citizens of Lake County, Florida—especially those of Eustis—know how to work, they know how to serve others less fortunate, and they know how to have fun. It was my privilege to live very much a John Boy Walton existence growing up in a small hometown. My classmates and I had the opportunity to be intensively involved in football and swimming and theater and music and more. It was up to us.

And we had the best teachers and coaches and pastors and friends' parents on earth in our cheering section. I didn't know it at the time, but I also received specific preparation for a career as a Marine Corps public affairs officer. I learned journalism from real newspaper people, including Al Palmer, George Perkins, Juanita Buca, and Marie Bolles, and I learned community relations from Troop 151 scoutmaster Clayton Bishop.

Esteemed cohorts from the U.S. Marine Corps Combat Correspondents Association have been a second family to me since I left home in 1972. Many are mentioned in these ten chapters, but I would also give a special shout-out to our current national president, Fred Lash, and our underpaid, overworked executive director, Jack Paxton (and his lovely bride, Pat, of Wildwood, Florida).

Thanks also to public affairs and college friends and advisers from Norfolk's Camp Elmore to Kentucky's Asbury College to the fjords of Norway—and everywhere in between.

Again, many are named in these pages—but all are named in my heart. Particular thanks to Dr. Brooks Hill, my mentor at Oklahoma University, now holding forth in San Antonio, where he chairs Trinity University's Communications Department.

My academic colleagues at the Defense Information School's Public Affairs Leadership Department are a joy to work with, and I received especially robust support and advice from Bob Jordan, James Jarvis, Dave Phillips, and from our commandant, Navy captain Curry Graham.

Finally, I thank the Lord for Ceresse, my bride of thirty-four years. Never impressed with "the things of this world," Coach Tom Comer's pretty, brown-eyed daughter could fry chicken, back in a horse trailer with one hand, and love children, grandchildren, and a husband the way children, grandchildren, and a husband need to be loved.

It is in her precious memory that this book is dedicated.

Chapter 1

IT STARTS WITH AN ATTITUDE

Getting Your Head in the Game

In peace there's nothing so becomes a man
As modest stillness and humility:
But when the blast of war blows in our ears,
Then imitate the action of the tiger.
— WILLIAM SHAKESPEARE, *HENRY V*

Chutzpah and humility. If your job is to tell the Marine Corps story, these are the two qualities you must possess in abundance. There's a time to lowball it, to let the other fellow do the talking, to let the Corps' deeds speak for themselves.

And there's a time to press the attack, with jeep-stealing, headline-grabbing, over-the-top creativity and relentless salesmanship.

Working at the media center in Qatar at the U.S. Central Command's forward headquarters during the start-up of Operation Iraqi Freedom (OIF) in January 2003, a young Marine major approached me, upset. "Sir, you've got to be the media spokesman here," he said. "Right now, Central Command plans to have a civilian and some Navy public affairs officers talking on camera. We need a Marine!"

I told him to relax, "because the Lord and the media love the Marines." And so they do, apparently. For starters, "OIF I" was an embedded journalists' war (to the natural frustration of some fine reporters—and their military public affairs counterparts—who were stuck in the rear with the gear).

To say that the U.S. Marines got their share of coverage is an understatement. Far outnumbered by units from the United States Army, the Leathernecks under the flag of the Camp Pendleton, California-based First Marine Expeditionary Force saw their combat exploits disproportionately broadcast far and wide. Such had been the case in Operation Desert Storm in 1991 and in the South Pacific in World War II, where the Army actually conducted many more amphibious landings than the Marines.

For the record, my own father was a soldier; I was born in the Panama Canal Zone and lived in Fort Stewart, Georgia, before Dad left the Army for opportunities during Florida's boom years of the 1950s and 1960s. So I'm not trying to denigrate the U.S. Army or anybody else. In fact, a tip o' the skimmer to the Army National Guard as I happily borrow one of their old marketing slogans for this chapter heading.

But the press loves us—that's just the way it is. During the early days of the war in Iraq, both embedded media and stateside editors and news directors were possessed with an almost in-bred cultural penchant for headlines and sound bytes that spoke of "the Marines."

And who can blame them?

America's Corps of Marines has inspired millions. The Marines' enviable combat record, spiffy dress blue uniforms, square-jawed ways, and steadfast adherence to their own lore and legacy are the stuff copy editors dream about.

All the Leathernecks have to do is continue to perform: take the hill, win the battle, feed the starving refugee, snuff out the forest fire, fill the sandbag . . . it doesn't matter. The deeds *will* be recorded—but with more fullness, accuracy, and consistency if the commands involved planning and executing an aggressive public affairs plan.

That's what this book is about: publicizing your organization *the Marine way.* That means gratefully acknowledging that, indeed, the Lord and the media *do* seem to like us—but tempering that enthusiasm with a healthy dose of the same institutional insecurity that drives Marines to think outside the box, to do more with less, and, always, to do it with vigor, boldness, and candor.

Depending on the size of your unit, you perhaps benefit from the fulltime services of an assigned public affairs officer—the PAO. Perhaps you have a hard-charging staff noncommissioned officer (NCO) or an NCO attached to your regiment or aircraft group. For a great many commands, however, telling the Marine Corps story is a collateral duty that falls on the shoulders of already-multihatted leaders on independent duty in cities or on college campuses all across the country. It's for those Marines, and to anyone new to public affairs, that this book is designed.

And it's for commanders, especially aspiring commanders—Marine leaders who, as they ascend the promotion ladder, are observing that "this public affairs stuff" has become increasingly important. The good news is that the same Marine traits that have brought you success thus far are precisely the same ones that will win the day in the public affairs arena.

Finally, *Command Attention* was written for my fellow students and practitioners of organizational communications from all walks of life, military and civilian. You'll see in these pages a penchant for culling ideas from all available sources; and it is my sincere hope that you would find herein at least a modicum of PR fodder as you chart your own unique vocational course.

The Three-Pronged Attack

Telling the Marine Corps Story is a campaign traditionally fought on three fronts:

1. Internal Information: reaching Marines and their families;
2. External Information: getting the news to the general public; and
3. Community Relations: unlike the other two prongs of the attack, it does not rely on a medium to carry the

message—this is the live, face-to-face stuff of which parades, speeches, air shows, and school visits are made.

In the case of Internal and External Information, the differentiation denotes the intended *audience*, not the means to reach that audience. In point of fact, once a story or photo is posted to the Web or appears in a base (or civilian) newspaper, it's "out there," anyway. The information is, by definition, both "internal" and "external."

Command newspapers and bulletin boards aside, the majority of active-duty family members live off base, and that certainly is the case for reservists, retirees, and civilian government and contracted employees who serve alongside Marines. Cooperating with civilian media outlets, then, is in the Marine Corps' best interest—we often rely on them to reach our own people with important information.

In fact, all three prongs work together routinely. They not only dovetail; as Lt. Gen. Marty Berndt once correctly emphasized to his public affairs staff, they're also concentric circles. It is difficult to imagine the issue or event that does not touch on all three functional areas.

For example, suppose your command hosts 8th and I's popular Battle Color Ceremony. Clearly, that's a community relations or "comrel" event. But you're going to invite people by both internal and external information vehicles—the same vehicles that will treat reading (or viewing, or listening) audiences to some postevent coverage.

Substance over Form

"Give me a sound check, we're about to go live."

"Have you seen today's front page?"

"Come quick: Daddy's on television!"

Yeah, it's fun, exciting work, accented by the sense of urgency and glamour that characterizes the news business (and show business, for that matter—perhaps less of a stretch than we'd like to admit). But it's seldom the most important work. That is done by the lance corporal on the line with a locked and loaded M-16 in his sweaty nineteen-year-old hands.

If the Marine Corps is a football team, the public affairs warrior is the placekicker. But the best kickers are clearly team players, even if their uniforms tend to stay cleaner than those of their teammates. This specialist hones his particular skills but does everything he can to be a functioning member of his team first—including being prepared to make the occasional open-field tackle.

In the motion picture *300,* the brave warrior King Leonidas, on the eve of what he knew would be his last, desperate battle, tells his de facto PAO, "Let's take a walk."

"You have another talent unlike any other Spartan," the king explains to Dilios, who protests the sovereign sending him back to the rear. "You will deliver my final orders to the council with force and verve.

"Tell them our story," Leonidas says. "Make every Greek know what happened here. You'll have a grand tale to tell."

When Dilios returned to Sparta, he successfully used his skills to accomplish his storytelling mission. He wasn't hung up about personal recognition, grabbing awards as the best battle journalist or copywriter of his day, nor was he even laboring to save his comrades; they were already destined to die. Rather, he saw his work as fitting in to a much loftier purpose: preserving his country and, beyond that, fighting for freedom for all men. Sounds a little like those time-honored words from the first stanza of the Marine hymn, eh? You know, "First to fight for right and freedom. . . ."

When I joined the Marines in 1972, the commandant of the Marine Corps still did not have a full seat with the Joint Chiefs of Staff, and the Corps was subject to the occasional, Trumanesque editorial that ostensibly asked, "Why is it again that we need a Marine Corps when we already have an Army—and an Air Force?"

There was a palpable undercurrent among my peers in public affairs of "what must we do to 'save' the Marine Corps," if it came to that. Heretically, perhaps, that was never a good enough reason for me to pour my total commitment and energy into the enterprise. Rather, I subscribe to the unvarnished take offered to then-commandant, Gen. Randolph McC. Pate by Lt. Gen. "Brute" Krulak, chronicled in the latter's classic tome, *First to Fight*: "While the functions which we discharge must always be done . . . in terms of cold mechanical logic, the United States does not *need* a Marine Corps. However, for good reasons which completely transcend cold logic, the United States *wants* a Marine Corps."

General Krulak goes on to state that "should the people ever lose that conviction—as a result of our failure to meet their high, almost spiritual standards—the Marine Corps will quickly disappear."

Even if working to save the institution from extinction was my goal, that's a strategic mission that would be out of my lane anyway—and certainly is far beyond the capabilities of even the most gifted public affairs professional.

Rather, I've happily chosen to seek help from above, as described by J. E. Seim in verse three of the classic naval hymn, "Eternal Father, Strong to Save":

Eternal Father, grant we pray
to all Marines, both night and day:
the courage, honor, strength and skill,
their land to serve, they law fulfill.
Be *Thou* the shield forevermore,
from every peril to the Corps.(italics mine)

I hope that, as you thumb through the pages of this offering, you'll see clearly that PAOing is a team sport and that you'll be needing to enlist all the help you can, divine and otherwise.

With that, let me echo Shakespeare's call, and bid ye "Go gentlemen, every man unto his charge!"

For Your Rucksack

Pride of ownership, pride of authorship can be a good thing—but those tasked with communicating the organization's mission, goals, history, and traditions need to hold personal pride loosely: the Marine Corps belongs to "us" and to "them." Good public affairs is not an "I" or "me" proposition.

You may have some particular ideas about the content of the base newspaper or closed-circuit television operation, for example. You should set and maintain professional standards, yes; but be mindful that it is "their" newspaper and TV station—not your own. These and other communication tools are designed to assist commanders and to help the Key Volunteer program do its good work. And youth sports. And the chaplain. And the rod and gun club.

Did I mention the retired community? And the civilian workforce?

Bottom line: If you will be a generous steward of the special assets to which you have been entrusted, you will be wildly successful. I guarantee it.

Chapter 2

TELLING IT TO THE MARINES

Internal Information

If the trumpet give forth an uncertain sound,
who will prepare for battle?

— I CORINTHIANS 14:8

etting "the word" to your own people is one of the most
critical (and challenging) tasks facing a leader—especially when it includes family members, the supporting
establishment, the retired community, and others.

But it can also be a lot of fun.

Does the boss use morning formations or e-mails or news-
letters or message traffic or town meetings or base television
to get the word out? The right answer, of course, is, "all of the
above"—and then some.

The Ubiquitous Base Newspaper

For an enthusiastic base commander, publishing a base newspaper or operating a local government television station is an
extension of his mayoral role. He and his staff have the opportunity to demonstrate attention-grabbing creativity and journalistic excellence with these and other tools—just as they
might in any mid-sized city in America.

"Internal" (the Army calls it "command") information
refers not so much to the tools used but to the intended audience, that is, "it's just 'us.'"

But what if most of your Marines live off base?

Again: if you're using commercial radio, television, and
local newspaper outlets to get info to your people, you are—by

definition—engaged in "external information." Command policy, sometimes articulated via direct quotes or on-air interviews with the commander, is now reaching the general public—and that's a good thing. Media consumers get a peek into Marine Corps culture when a unit prepares to deploy, for instance; they can take pride and some comfort in the fact that their Marine Corps regards this as very serious business, that military authorities are transparent in their desire to ensure, for example, that Marines' wills and powers of attorney are in order; that their families' housing situation is "good to go"; and that their vehicles are safely stored.

If your base newspaper is circulated "out in town" (it should be, if that's where a majority of your warriors reside), those same messages are reaching both our internal and external publics—and you are, indeed, telling your unfiltered Marine Corps story, to everybody, on at least a weekly basis.

To have any chance of being believed by Marines or by their civilian neighbors, your publication can't look like a "military newspaper." Rather, it needs the look and feel of, well, a "newspaper." Will it spout the party (command) line? Sure it will, as expected—just as reliably as the *Washington Times* rallies behind right-wing causes and the *Baltimore Sun* leans left.

But that doesn't keep them, or you, from demonstrating journalistic professionalism, including good writing, eye-catching photography, and a colorful sports section. The Marines assigned to produce that newspaper have, after all, received college credit for courses received at Defense Information School (www.dinfos.osd.mil; more on their training in chapter 6). And, like their civilian counterparts, they compete annually for nationwide, even worldwide, recognition in all categories of writing, photography, layout, and design.

TV, Radio, and More

The same high standards and audience appeal should apply to other internal information media as well, be it television, radio, or a command Web site.

Television

When a cable television company wins the contract to provide services to the living quarters on your base, a commander's access channel is generally part of the deal. At a bare minimum, this gives the commanding officer, the CO, the ability to run an electronic scroll, updating it during weather and other emergencies, or even to go on camera for special announcements.

You can do more.

Why not make that scroll a jazzed-up PowerPoint presentation, with great photography (readily available to you from your own staff, combat camera, and via http://dodimagery. afis.osd.mil)? Your "slides" can be shout-outs, recognizing the Marine of the Month, the newly elected president of the Senior Noncommissioned Officers' Wives Club, or the intramural football champions.

Background music? Your base audiovisual folks will have some licensed, generic elevator music—but why not go one better? At Camp Lejeune, we worked with the Chamber of Commerce to identify local radio stations whose music would be appropriate for this cost-free, win-win situation. We spread the wealth by alternating the signal and stayed away from those stations that played suggestive lyrics or displayed shock-jock antics (that "good order and discipline" clause comes in mighty handy).

Here's a handy secret: there are more trained broadcasters in the Marine Corps than there are slots for them at forward-based Armed Forces Radio and Television Stations. That means you likely have on your staff a combat correspondent who is already comfortable in the studio—to say nothing of the massive pool of volunteers available to you from every quarter.

And even if you don't have a television camera, the amount of public access programming available to you is staggering. At Camp Lejeune, we did the legal homework that allowed us also to ask major film studios for a one-time use of a particular film. The worst they can do is say no. Same with NFL Films, music video producers, and a host of other possibilities.

Don't have a TV operation at all? Arrange for your Marines to be regular guests on local morning talk shows, much the same way you see the state trooper appearing to explain the new window tinting law or to promote highway safety for the coming holiday weekend.

Radio

The same philosophy and mutual agreements used for television apply—and then some.

Radio "beepers" are easy: all you need is a telephone, and you can basically have an overseas conversation with any DJ or radio news director in America. Best to scratch out a few notes beforehand, making sure you have a good grasp of the facts you wish to report, along with some "color." How's morale? What's the weather like? How was the trip over?

More foolproof, and easier to execute, is to simply write up a scripted thirty- or sixty-second spot. Phone your contact and read it over the air. You can even leave it on voice mail (having coordinated with the station beforehand).

Back in the rear, how about offering up one of your combat correspondents to do a drive-time base update on a local radio station?

Consider the variety of formats and audiences, and market your ideas accordingly. In Jacksonville, North Carolina, Mel Bland owns and manages an AM gospel station. On Friday mornings he was pleased to host the thirty-minute *Joshua Report*, an interview with one of our Navy chaplains (or a Marine leader who was a strong man or woman of faith).

Web Sites

One of my first jobs upon retiring from the Marines was serving as a civilian public affairs officer, standing up an operation that had not been "on the books" for nearly a decade. Pioneering has its own special appeal—and when you're starting from ground base zero, any initiative you take looks like magic and is well appreciated by an organization previously starved for information and recognition.

Part of the kick was introducing a new, colorful Web site; but I warned my enthusiastic (and only) assistant: "Be careful what you wish for—we've just inherited a daily newspaper." In other words, expectations would be high for keeping that new site fresh and accurate.

You can go a long way toward staying ahead of the bow wave by partnering with stakeholders, letting them take responsibility for maintaining content in their areas of interest and expertise. And you have a treasure trove of public domain imagery at your fingertips (perhaps displayed in slide show form or some other revolving method), starting with the crisp action photography that's refreshed daily on www.usmc.mil.

Finally, the opportunity to automate has never been better; it's common practice for Web sites to offer scrolling news updates that pertain to their area, for example. And the electrons do all the work.

Whatever It Takes

Your job is getting the word out—don't get hung up on means. In my younger years, I thought the base marquee was rather a pain to deal with. But who better to "own" it than the PAO? In addition to posting timely information about the weather closing or coming change of command, it gives him the ability to market the *other* internal media.

In Jacksonville, the Camp Lejeune *Globe* was featured on billboards—at no cost to the Marine Corps (and at great benefit to the willing civilian publisher, whose livelihood depended on awareness of his product and subsequent paid advertising in it).

Volunteers who helped us fill the pages of our base newspaper earned "I Was Published in the *Globe*" T-shirts, provided by the Marine Corps Community Services Directorate (with their logo proudly silk-screened on the back).

Context is everything. Our friend and fellow Chamber of Commerce member, Jamie Lanier, owns Tire Country at the busy intersection of Jacksonville's Highway 24 and Western Boulevard (think "Times Square"). A unit homecoming message or congratulations on a Marine's individual accomplishment posted on the towering Tire Country marquee was always sure to get noticed.

Where do people gather? Where do people *wait?* Is your base newspaper available at the doctor's office? Will the folks who run the mess hall or bowling alley agree to set their television channels to your station, at least for part of the day?

External Media

Once again, you're not just talking to the general public; you are also talking to your own Marines when you go on camera or grant that print interview. Which is another reason to welcome, not avoid, the civilian news media, *especially* in time of crisis—and especially in time of after-hours crisis. You are sending appropriate messages to your own people— messages of compassion, swift reaction, command attention, and concern. Should the members of the command wait for the weekly base rag when they can get it "from the horse's mouth" on the radio, the 11 o'clock news, or next morning's daily newspaper?

Before one of your staff members deploys to support exercises or operations, make sure the local television station receives a decent head-and-shoulders shot of your Marine combat correspondent (in the uniform he'll be wearing "over there"). He can then call in reports, packed with local names and updates on the home-based units. The producer will throw his picture on the screen and a map from his current location—and families will have one more emotional lifeline to their loved ones. In so doing, you will have demonstrated yet another excellent example of *external* media reaching both external *and internal* audiences.

Touting Unsung Heroes

Dr. Linda Keaton-Lima's forthcoming book, *War Is Not Just for Heroes,* has it right. Marine Corps public affairs, to a large extent, should support the little guy; the unheralded; the overlooked; the smaller, unique organizations on your base; and the other Service contingents you probably host. The list goes on.

You won't get all those hardworking Americans on the cover of *Time,* and many of those groups simply will not be as important to the local civilian media as they are to their commander (and to your commander's public affairs ninjas!).

But *you* can publicize their contributions with virtually unlimited internal media venues, many of which are under your shop's direct control. What a grand opportunity to give credit where it's due, to affect morale, even to raise the reenlistment rate.

Never disdain the lists and statistics that are sometimes relegated to small print, such as the base school honor roll, youth soccer results, and new graduates from the NCO Academy. Tiny type or not, this is the stuff that gets underlined and taped to somebody's refrigerator.

Is the *Marine Corps Times* going to mention your high shooters from last week on the rifle range? Will ESPN be talking about the sergeant who made the all-Marine basketball team? Will *Business Week* profile the civil servant who just returned from a professional conference in Atlanta? *That's where you and your staff come in, right?*

The Hierarchy of (Internal) News

Pete Williams, a newsman friend who deployed with our Second Force Service Support Group in the early stages of

Operation Iraqi Freedom, today edits the *Richmond County Daily Journal* in Rockingham, North Carolina. He shared with me an insightful story about his first day on the job at his first newspaper. It was in Mount Airy, in the highlands country of Carolina the town folks said Andy Griffith's *Mayberry RFD* was modeled after.

Back in the early 1970s when Pete started out, it was not uncommon on network television news to see a set of wall clocks showing the time in New York, Los Angeles, London, and Tokyo. The idea, of course, was to give viewers the impression that they were getting a worldwide perspective of the day's events.

In Mount Airy, however, Pete saw a different set of clocks. Hanging over the editor's desk were clocks labeled Dobson, Pilot Mountain, Ararat, and Mount Airy.

The *Mount Airy News'* latest hire got the message: This newspaper was committed to a readership that held dear its local ties. Any story emanating from overseas; Washington, D.C.; or even the state capital in Raleigh had best have a clear tie back to the people and events of Mount Pilot.

Similarly, a command newspaper editor can't have an attitude of "all the news that fits, we print." At Camp Lejeune, we used a hierarchy of news.

The ideal story featured a Camp Lejeune-based Marine or sailor or was judged to be of great personal, localized interest to him or her. Other "stars" in that constellation included family members, civil servants, area retirees, and—in descending order—local, regional, and state news. On those occasions when we did delve into national or international news, it was *always with a local tie*.

We also had a few placards posted in the newspaper office's spaces, much like the motivational sayings you might find in a football locker room. Chief among them was one that read, "LOCAL, LOCAL, LOCAL."

For Your Rucksack

Congratulations, media mogul! If you're the PAO at some of our bases and commands, you now find yourself in charge of a weekly newspaper, a Web site, and both a radio and TV operation.

What a magnificent opportunity to train and develop your staff! And unlike your college friend who entered civilian news management, you don't have to worry about salaries or cost of newsprint, or the electric bill. You are free to spend your creative capital on producing and marketing a product that young Americans will want to read, or watch, or listen to.

You could half-step it, and maybe nobody will notice. Such are the tepid expectations of most organizational information vehicles, both in and outside the military. But if you really want a challenge, try getting inside that young lance corporal's head. Consumption of media is a very personal act, beginning with the choice to even pick up a particular periodical or set your automobile radio button to a favorite station.

The company gunny might be able to yell, "Listen up!" at morning formation with mostly positive results—but the PAO cannot compel another human being to read the base newspaper or surf the command Web site.

Yet, the stakes are pretty high. Will your shop produce the story that gets young Marines thinking about road fatigue? Can your staff put a dent in the suicide rate? Will somebody miss out on a reenlistment bonus because your treatment of the issue didn't grab him? Will a Marine's new bride not know about readily available family support as her husband ships out in harm's way? Will a combat-decorated retiree or widow miss a policy change that affects disability or pension?

If you take up the gauntlet, you'll derive an additional benefit: You'll gain tremendous insight into the world of the civilian news media (see next chapter). Deadlines, fact-checking and competing priorities are now a regular part of *your* daily routine, just as it is theirs. Reading about journalism and talking to news people is one thing—but there's no better means than *doing it* for gaining solid understanding.

Chapter 3

REACHING "THE PUBLIC"

External Information

> The future success of the Marine Corps depends on two factors: first, an efficient performance of all the duties to which its officers and men may be assigned; second, promptly bringing this efficiency to the attention of the proper officials of the government, and the American people.
>
> — LT. GEN. JOHN A. LEJEUNE

H opefully, we've convinced you that relations with the civilian news media do not constitute the be-all and end-all of public affairs. That said, make no mistake: this aspect—this reaching the general public *through an independent medium*—is, to borrow the infantry's moniker, "the queen of battle."

If you could only have one of the three prongs in our "three-pronged attack," this is it. The bottom-line reason America has a military public affairs capability is to get the civilian journalist to the battlefield and, when necessary, to assist the civilian journalist in getting her story out.

Why? The civilian journalist generally has a much bigger microphone than you do—a much broader and quicker reach. More important, he has the credibility that comes only from independent reporting. At the end of the day, your PAO's report, as accurate and exciting as it may be, is still the word of a "government spokesman."

Remember, you need that civilian reporter for your internal information program, too; his reports—not yours—will more quickly and credibly reach family members (and even servicemen back in the rear), whether it's the college-educated Marine wife back in Yuma, Arizona, or that warrior's parents in Duluth, Minnesota. Your implied task, then, is to work *with* the civilian journalist, getting him the information he needs and, in so doing, achieving at least some level of success in getting *your* (command) message(s) in the report he files.

It could be argued that, especially with today's technology, a field commander is able to reach family members with unfiltered information via family grams, a constantly refreshed Web site, recorded command updates via telephone, and the like. True enough—but you're still not going to have the consistent, blanketed reach nor the credibility of the fourth estate, which has been at its first amendment chore as long as the Marines have been part of "providing for the common defense."

The operative word in "media relations," then, is the same key term you would choose from the phrases "community relations" or "foreign relations." Marines are good at *"relations"*—that's why we generally do well on recruiting duty, joint duty, foreign area officer duty, legislative duty, and other jobs where getting along with folks is paramount.

Care and Feeding

Establishing Relationships

In this era of e-mail, texting, and other seemingly efficient (but largely impersonal) communications, face-to-face is still very much appreciated—and that's your preference—for introducing yourself to the journalists who will be covering your command's activities.

A straight, brief office call is acceptable—just be mindful of your opposite number's deadlines and other time constraints. Like you, some times of day (and days of the week) are better than others.

If you can make him a cup of coffee or a breakfast or lunch, so much the better. And the very best scenario is to bring some nonurgent materials with you, perhaps an announcement you'd like to get in the paper or on the radio concerning the coming Fightin' 6th Marines reunion. If he's coming to you, perhaps you take him on a short drive, pointing out the new weapons simulator. Certainly you introduce him to your staff.

A small group lunch at the Officers or Staff Noncommissioned Officers Club is acceptable, too. Media folks are like most folks: they like to eat lunch and they appreciate being invited. You realize some efficiencies in a group setting—but strive for one-on-one opportunities to the greatest extent possible.

For some accurate, and enjoyable, insight into "their world," several movies are worth renting, including *Broadcast News,* Holly Hunter's acclaimed portrayal of a workaholic television producer, with John Hurt and Albert Brooks; and *The Paper,* a somewhat lighter story about New York City's gritty, manic newspaper competition starring Michael Keaton, Glenn Close, and Robert Duvall. *Absence of Malice,* a journalism ethics story featuring a thinly disguised *Miami Herald* and starring Paul Newman and Sally Field, is also quite good.

And when you get to know journalists for real, especially in a war zone, you're in for a treat. You will meet many reporters whose experience, bravery, eccentricities, and work ethic will blow you away. Like you, they don't do it for the money.

Maj. Dan McSweeney's observation about their commitment and professionalism applies: "We're more alike than different," Gunga Dan asserts. "We fight; they write."

Maintaining Relationships

Call once in a while when you *don't* want something. Compliment him or her on a piece of nonmilitary reporting you've seen on television or in the newspaper. Differentiate between the "beat reporter" and the sojourner. Is the beat reporter, your local guy, special? You bet he is.

Somebody in your media group is probably regarded as the "dean" or is, at least, the most experienced of the bunch. Nothing wrong with having your commanding general recognize him first. (Yep, just like Helen Thomas at those White House press conferences.)

Let 'em vent with you occasionally, and be patient and courteous when they feel compelled to phone you in the evenings or on weekends.

There was a particular photographer I worked with who called twice on Sunday afternoons to complain about an issue. It could have waited—and my colleagues told me he had a reputation for stirring up trouble. But I listened to him, I got him the answers he needed, and I kept it friendly.

When I got transferred a couple years later, he surprised me at my going-away soiree with a beautifully framed, artsy photograph depicting a sunset view from the front of our headquarters building. The picture's hanging in my study as I tap this out, smiling.

Consider Special Access

Working with the Base Provost Marshal at Camp Lejeune a few years ago, we were able to get special passes for the military beat reporters who covered us. They appreciated the courtesy and the streamlined access. And why not? Those who cover the military nationally have offices inside the Pentagon; and when reporters are embedded with us overseas, they're with us 24/7.

Query Procedures

Common courtesy is your best guide here. When a reporter calls or e-mails, respond promptly. Ascertain what, exactly, she's after—and try to get it for her. A simple "query sheet," executed electronically or otherwise, is the standard way to efficiently handle the information request. You want to make sure you're telling everybody the same thing, and you want to be sure to include everybody on periodic updates. Don't worry: they'll be calling you; but good customer service and Marine pride should drive you to beat 'em to the punch when you can.

Pitching and Marketing Stories

You're always going to have your elevator speech—a commercial—in your cargo pocket; we're talking just two or three quick bullets from which you enthusiastically describe to a reporter, editor, or news director why this is a story worth pursuing. (You actually want to have *several* elevator speeches at the ready, covering a variety of topics that serve to support one or more of your command's overall goals.)

So much the better if you provide backup—maybe a news release with photograph, or at least a fact sheet. That way the reporter not only goes forward with your suggested story, but you've also given him some meaty statistics and other substantive information to round out his story. The easier you can make it for him, the better. Plus, you've now got a basic product you can customize for a boatload of other media.

On the soft feature front at Camp Lejeune, I got in the habit of having a brief Monday morning visit or a phone call with the local military writer for the (Jacksonville) *Daily News.* I gave him about ten new story ideas each week. With a combined military, civil service, and family member population that exceeded 150,000, it wasn't hard. He used many of them. And he was a happy camper—which didn't hurt matters when I needed to request a correction or offer a clarification on a quote I'd bobbled in a hard news story.

Another marketplace for you is the letters-to-the-editor column. Once I wrote in to correct a newspaper on referring to an artillery battery as an artillery *company*—an honest enough mistake. But I took the opportunity to point out our local artillery regiment's current, far-flung deployment schedule and the Corps' history of morphing artillerymen into provisional rifle companies in Grenada and elsewhere. Sure made our PA shop popular with the cannon cockers.

The Media Encounter

Preparation

OK, you're going to conduct your first media interview. Or you're going to prep your boss for an interview. For some, the media interview, and particularly when it's television, is the seminal event.

In reality, it is a conversation. Granted, it is a conversation witnessed by others, sometimes millions. But it is a conversation, nonetheless. While you're mindful of the audience you are reaching through a medium, you want to focus on the individual with whom you are speaking. What the larger audience will then discern is sincerity and respect.

Even in very public interactions, sometimes *how* we say it is at least as important as *what* we say. So shape the battlefield to facilitate a productive and courteous exchange. Be on time. Be friendly. Ensure ease of access and logistics support, when necessary. Exchange biographies beforehand. Let the reporter know your "rules of engagement," perhaps limiting yourself to the subject at hand, alerting him ahead of time which areas might be off limits because of security or legal concerns, and so forth.

And practice. Have another staff member "murder board" you. It helps you make sure you know your stuff. One popular method is the "3x5," in which you craft responses to five questions that she'll probably ask, five that you wish she would ask, and five that you hope she does not ask.

Even if one of those unpleasant questions seems totally bizarre or you know that you are constrained from answering it, at least you won't be surprised. And, more important, you won't *look* surprised.

Execution

You know your stuff—that's why the reporter wants to talk to you (or your commander, or the subject matter expert who has been "voluntold"). And now you know your interviewer. You're ready to engage!

You'll do more than just fine if you'll follow a handful of very simple rules:

1. Don't speculate; stick to the facts.
2. Stay in your lane; don't talk above your billet, pay grade, or area of expertise.
3. Don't be afraid to say "I don't know."
4. Take your time in forming your answers! Except for the stereotypical, sweaty palms, *60 Minutes* gotcha interviews—generally reserved for corporate crooks and polygamists—your lengthy pauses will never make it on TV or radio (and would very rarely be described in a print story).
5. Tell the truth.
6. If you can't divulge an answer because of security considerations, just say so. Never fall back on "no comment."

Beyond that, don't hesitate to work in some command messages or name names, including the unit or civilian agency that helped in the rescue, Toys for Tots drive, or homecoming event.

Got a special point or two you want to make? That might be the time when you very intentionally use the reporter's name, especially in a broadcast interview. ("Well, Mary, this is probably the most capable combat jet in the arsenal.")

And don't let the reporter put words in your mouth. If you've been asked the equivalent of the proverbial "When did you stop beating your wife?" those are not the words you want to use in your answer. Better: "Actually, Bill, Marine Corps values serve to support and strengthen families."

After Care

The interview is not over until you see the media drive away. More than one prematurely relaxed senior officer has been caught off guard during that time when the media is packing up and everybody is saying their good-byes. In the case of broadcast interviews, sometimes you are still being recorded.

As soon as they *do* leave, the PAO has some immediate responsibilities. He should provide a first-impressions critique of his boss' interview performance (along with an educated prediction on how the story will be portrayed). He needs to back-brief his higher headquarters PAO. He'll want to phone the reporter soon after to ascertain what further information might be provided. If the reporter is willing to provide feedback, including constructive criticism of your performance or any aspect of her visit, that is news you can use.

Don't ask for a copy of the broadcast interview. That's your job. But do find out when it will air or when the print story will run and take the extra step of getting that product in the hands of all interested parties (with a handwritten thank-you note to the subject matter expert who drew the short straw).

Maj. Steve Cox was a master at feedback when he was the first PAO for the Joint Task Force (JTF) Horn of Africa in 2002. On a daily basis, he produced an electronic roll-up of news stories that featured the JTF and e-mailed it to every warrior in the entire organization.

When "Bad News" Strikes

First off, bad news is *not* like fine wine: it does not get better with age. It is more like a dead fish: the longer you (try to) hide it in a drawer, the more it stinks.

Ret. Col. Tom Fields, a Vietnam-era director of public affairs who carved out an enviable reputation for innovation and boldness, was adamant that the Marine Corps look at our public-perception wins and losses like a baseball season, not a football schedule. "We're big enough and strong enough," he said, "to absorb some hits.

"Besides," he stressed, "we can't have it both ways. If we want the accolades for our battle successes and gentlemanly conduct on the parade field in our dress blues, we have to quickly and forthrightly address the inevitable bar fights, as well."

Torie Clarke, the assistant secretary of defense for public affairs through 9/11, the initial deployment to Afghanistan, and during the first phase of Operation Iraqi Freedom, got it right when she titled her 2006 book, *Lipstick on a Pig*. You can't (or shouldn't) attempt to spin, minimize, dress up, or otherwise make pretty the inevitable bad news.

In the military, especially, trust and integrity demand public accountability. "Maximum Disclosure—Minimum Delay" is the mantra taught at Defense Information School and, except where legitimate security concerns dictate otherwise, the PAO's job is to "get it out there"—fast.

Generally, our citizens are understanding of a screwup; but Americans look with great disdain on a *cover*-up.

The news sometimes will be ugly—and why would it be otherwise, since we're in the business of killing bad guys and blowing things up? We do inherently dangerous work, every day, even in peacetime. There's a reason why many insurance companies don't look fondly on their civilian clients piloting airplanes (much less routinely jumping from them).

Add the fact that the Armed Forces we represent number a million plus, each a human being capable of doing or saying the wrong thing. Leadership and training notwithstanding, the inevitability of what we call "bad news" becomes quite clear.

The best commands deal with bad news quickly, and in the case of alleged crimes and misconduct, usually put out two boilerplate messages:

(a) the alleged offenses, if they occurred, are taken very seriously and certainly run counter to Marine Corps policy and our longstanding tradition of courage, honor, and commitment.

(b) our investigation, which has already been initiated, will be fair and thorough, in accordance with regulations and the Uniformed Code of Military Justice.

In other words: we're on it, but let us not rush to judgment.

For Your Rucksack

Love on the media "grunts," to. The on-air reporter or bylined print journalist is "the star" and generally gets much more attention than that given his colleagues—for example, the photographer, videographer, or sound man

But these workhorses of the media, the technicians who really make it all work, warrant your attention. Besides having names and families and hometowns, they have some legitimate professional concerns that need attention. In a press conference situation, for example, have you arranged adequate line-of-sight for the still photographers? Is scaffolding appropriate? Or maybe a shooters' pit such as you might see during Senate hearings, where a bevy of photographers is seated right in front of the lawmakers' bench?

What about the sound? Do the techies have special acoustics issues that you might be able to help with? Are power outlets readily available for klieg lights?

In sum, don't go gaga over the celebrity journalist with whom you'll be dealing. Certainly treat him with courtesy and respect as a fellow pro, but never at the expense of his "grunts" and certainly *never* at the expense of your local gaggle. They are your bread and butter.

Chapter 4

GOING FACE TO FACE

Community Relations

Much have I seen and known; cities of men and manners, climates, councils, governments . . . I am a part of all that I have met.

— LORD TENNYSON, *ULYSSES*

One intuitive feeling he had . . . was that a Marine commander should establish a good rapport with civilian population of the local town.

— PAT CONROY, *THE GREAT SANTINI*

What makes community relations so special, Col. Fred Peck used to say, is that you get "just one chance to do it right." Unlike the television or newspaper interview, which can be amended or explained in subsequent editions, this face-to-face part of public affairs doesn't have a rewind button. Be it a speech, parade, or static display at a local festival, that singular event may be the only time some of our citizens are able to see their Marines "live and in person."

When he commanded the Second Marine Division at Camp Lejeune, Maj. Gen. John Sattler met personally with any Marines who were scheduled to represent the Corps "out in public" that weekend—even if it was four-man amtrac crew, led by a corporal, setting up at the Sneads Ferry Shrimp Festival.

Of course, if the command's internal information program is a strong one, and if at least rudimentary media training is part of the external information program, such "confirmation briefs" are practically pro forma—just a reminder to be squared away, friendly, and courteous. But what a clear message Sattler's meetings sent to all concerned, that the excursion was important to the commanding general!

Opportunities Abound

What community relations events might you be involved with?

Parades

"Everybody loves a parade," the old saying goes—and it still applies today. Check out the U.S. Marine Corps presence in Macy's Thanksgiving Day Parade—or in the Tournament of Roses extravaganza on New Year's Day (where the local Marine Reserve for years hosted a postparade reception that was regarded as the hottest ticket in town).

Locally, you may be asked to provide a senior commander waving from a jeep or convertible. Or, as was the case in South Carolina's Lowcountry last year, the Air Station CO walked the Water Festival Parade route with his family, stopping frequently to greet their fellow citizens in military-friendly Beaufort. So the parade isn't always about just the band or the tactical vehicles. Just ask those out West who line the street to cheer the well-muscled palominos of the Mounted Color Guard from Marine Corps Logistics Base, Barstow, California.

When scheduling participation, especially if the event is in a smaller town or rural area, you don't want to make your judgment on projected numbers alone. Remember, you own the tools to garner some follow-on publicity.

A word of caution: temper organizers' expectations. Well-meaning community or veterans groups sometimes have to be schooled on the availability (or lack thereof) of your musical units, rolling stock, and, especially, troops in formation. We're in demand, especially around Christmas, Veteran's Day, and the 4th of July. It won't be unusual to field competing requests for the same date. I've even seen requests courtesy copied to an organizer's congressman, adding an extra step to the paperwork, since now what you'll have is a "congressional inquiry."

Many local military bands use "block leave" as a prudent measure to take care of their people; it's useful to the PAO to know those periods of nonavailability. It's sometimes your job, too, to explain that you can't support a parade with "marching troops" because of their operational tempo. An old Army boss used to kid about the special challenge of earnest parade organizers who would say to the commanding general, in effect, "please have your soldiers give up their weekend and put on a parade for us, so we can show them how much we appreciate them."

Music

If you've got access to a Marine Corps band or drum and bugle corps, congratulations. Those horns and snares and dress uniforms still make a splash wherever they appear, and, often as not, that unit is the "star of the show." A more detailed discussion of *the* Marine Band and the Drum and Bugle Corps, both based in our nation's capital, can be found in the next chapter, but any U.S. Marine Corps musical unit is a plum for grateful event organizers in cities and towns all over America. While your full band can put on a great concert, the unit invariably will boast smaller ensembles that might cater to country, jazz, or rock and roll listeners.

Maintain close contact with your command's musical unit, to include publicizing their schedule of appearances and offering your insight on venues and sponsoring organizations. At some commands, the band is part of the public affairs apparatus. And in the U.S. Air Force, bandsmen actually share the same overall military occupational specialty as writers, photographers, and broadcasters. To salesmen (read: recruiters), it's all about getting your "brand" out there, whether through words, pictures, or music.

By the way, you'd do well to make acquaintance with leaders from other area musical units, including high-school and sometimes community or veterans' marching bands; it's nice to be able to at least offer other possibilities when your command has to say no.

School Visits

Home-from-the-war speeches and classroom presentations have seen a natural resurgence of late, joining guest reader programs, volunteer coaching, and one-on-one tutoring. Chances are Marines are already doing these things in your area—you might have the easy job of just getting the word out. Other very natural reasons for getting out to the schoolhouse include assistance rendered the Junior Naval or Marine Corps ROTC Unit or perhaps demonstrating Marine Corps physical fitness or martial arts training to PE classes.

Worship Services

While it would be callous and commercial to suggest church as a recruiting or public relations venue, the fact is, our service members' participation in their respective houses of worship has always sent a clear, resonant message about Marine Corps values. Defense Department regulations are quite clear in authorizing general officers and other Marines to speak from the pulpit for special days set aside for patriotic observances. And it's simply a fact of life that numerous Marines are routinely heavily involved in their churches or synagogues in a very visible way from ushering to leading music and even sometimes to pastoring.

I always thought that internal and external stories on these twice-dedicated Marines were well received, especially by many of America's parents and grandparents who took comfort in knowing that their Leatherneck served in an organization well represented by God-fearing leaders.

Tactical Displays and Demonstrations

Youngsters still say "Cool!" when a military convoy passes the family on the interstate—so it's not surprising that even one Humvee or light-armored vehicle will be a hit at a community event. But it won't be the machinery that will capture citizens' interest—it will be the Marines in uniform. Take a cue from Lieutenant General Sattler and properly prepare your Marines for the gig: load them down with pamphlets and brief them on decorum, enthusiasm, courtesy, and so forth. And develop some sort of after-action mechanism so your command will have a feel for how it went, including the approximate number who visited your display at the fair or carnival.

Athletic Events

If the community that prays together, stays together (see "Worhip Services"), so, too, does the community that *plays* together. Golf outings and tournaments, softball games, equestrian events, road races . . . all these, and more, are proven winners for reaching out to our civilian neighbors. Use your imagination and steal promotional ideas wholesale from elsewhere. Can you arrange for a local Marine, fresh home from combat, to do the coin toss at the football game or toss out the first pitch on the baseball diamond? Or maybe your commanding general plays host to the mayor at the base intramural soccer championships, or rodeo, or boxing tournament.

Ceremonies

Changes of command, retirements, and special commemorative events (your base's 100th anniversary, for instance) are outstanding opportunities to bring civilians to your base.

Same with sendoffs and homecomings. They're obviously special times for family members, but such events are also ideal for inviting local officials and sports and entertainment celebrities—not for speechmaking and entertainment but to rub shoulders with America's real heroes. Certainly the Marine Corps League, VFW, and American Legion should be welcome—and don't discourage them if they'd like to show up with their barbeque or fish frying equipment.

A special note about local "VIPs." Command relationships with elected officials, city management, and chamber
leaders are to be nurtured and appreciated—but they're not
the only citizens with influence. Think about opening up that
aperture to include preachers, teachers, and others who might
not otherwise be on your command's regular guest list. It's
their Marine Corps, too. And you'd be giving them a very positive, patriotic experience to share with their many parishio-
ners, students, and friends.

Funerals

Certainly a funeral or a memorial service is not a festive "community relations event" in the classic sense—but the solemn
requirement to get it "just right" is particularly important.
Whether your role is as speaker, pallbearer, or member of the
color guard, or you are simply paying condolences, your uniform appearance and bearing must be poster perfect.

Speeches

Whether you're the speaker, the speechwriter, or the Marine who
sets up the gig (or perhaps all three!), the time-trusted podium
still provides a key venue for transmitting your message.

Getting out on the stump is easier than you might think.
Personal visits to the local Chamber of Commerce and a
couple veterans organizations should get the ball rolling.
Introduce yourself and let them know that you or your boss
(and, no doubt, others in your command) are available to local
program chairpersons who have speaking dates to fill.

What do you talk about? For starters, your duties. And
nobody knows them better than you. Say you're the inspec-
tor-instructor (the famous "I&I," in Marine Corps parlance).
You're tasked with advising and training, say, a company-sized
unit in a specific MOS. You are active duty, but those who are
depending on your guidance and current knowledge are reservists, including the CO. It's a unique and interesting arrangement,

and chances are Joe Civilian at the local Rotary Club had no idea about all the nuances you can share with the audience.

You are, essentially, a missionary evangelist for your job specialty as well as for the Marine Corps and, particularly, for the Marine Reserve.

In speaking about the Corps itself, you'll find it easy enough to get supporting materials from your higher headquarters' public affairs offices, up to and including the Corps' Division of Public Affairs at the Pentagon. Thanks to e-mail and the Web, they can backstop you almost instantaneously with talking points, transcripts of recent speeches, or congressional testimony from the commandant and other senior leaders, PowerPoint slides, and Ooorah! DVDs.

But be careful. The "pie in the sky" you get from the flagpole is meant only to augment your locally connected remarks. The last thing you want to deliver is a generic oratory that fails to consider your specific audience. I attended a banquet on the West Coast a few years ago during which a new brigadier general from Headquarters Marine Corps "put a check in the block" with thirty minutes of accurate statements on strategy and policy that had listeners rolling their eyeballs. In this case, attendees were largely well-read, currently engaged professional communicators with Marine Corps backgrounds. They already knew this stuff. The general missed an opportunity to get specific—and to favorably impress new friends in the process.

If you're new to this, you may want to write out your remarks, word for word, for your first few speeches—not to ultimately *deliver* your address *verbatim,* but so that you won't be mentally searching for that word or phrase that captures what you're trying to say.

When I served as aide-de-camp to the commanding general of the 4th Marine Aircraft Wing, my boss used a "necking-down" technique that proved effective for him. He had me first draft a regular manuscript (in this case, for an event in Pensacola). Once he was happy with the words, subsequent copies were printed with the text on the left half of the page only. The right side of the page contained just one paragraph that encapsulated what was on the left side. Follow-on "editions" always included the full text on the left side, but the right-side paragraph was whittled down to just a couple of sentences and, finally, just a phrase or two.

He wasn't concerned with perfect memorization, but with each iteration, he naturally becomes more and more familiar with his themes and content.

By the time Maj. Gen. Greg Corliss got in front of his audience a week later, he was down to an index card with a half-dozen key points, and he didn't even use the card as, hands on hips, he gave our Corps' newest, gold-winged pilots a memorable and motivating welcome into Marine Air.

As for the speaking itself, typical textbooks categorize "speeches to inform," "speeches to entertain," "speeches to persuade," and sometimes a half-dozen other categories.

I disagree.

While every speech may not be designed to sell your audience on a new weapon system or high-impact operational policy, the fact is, *all* your speeches will be speeches to persuade. If nothing else, you're trying to persuade your audience to *listen* to you.

Others have used simple, self-explanatory plans of attack to help them prepare and execute the public speaking mission, such as the 3 P's (Plan, Package, and Practice), the 3 Be's (Be Bold, Be Brief, and Be Gone), and the 3 Up's (Stand Up, Speak Up, and Shut Up).

Another method calls for spending maximum time on crafting an introduction and a conclusion that are "just right" and then making sure that those two elements are as close to one another as possible!

Butterflies Are a Good Thing

Professional speakers and entertainers will tell you that a little nervous energy is to be expected (if not, indeed, valued!). I love the opening lines from the Kenny Chesney song, "Never Gonna Feel Like That Again" in which he sings about "Friday night butterflies" before his high school football games and being "nervous 'til the kickoff came."

So it is with public speaking. You can feed off that nervousness—and release much of it with a robust, striking first few words. Sticking with Kenny's football analogy, I personally like to go with an onsides kick on the opening play. Surprise your audience, if you can! Open up with a loud, clear rendition of some warrior poetry, for example. It need not be the whole work, just a few lines from Kipling's "Gunga Din" or Shakespeare's *Henry V*—or even Rupertus' "This Is My Rifle."

Notes or Not?

I was most blessed to have spent my last five years on active duty at Camp Lejeune, launching pad for the worldwide travel and adventure activities of the Second Marine Expeditionary Force. During 1999–2004, at least, the culture in the command was "no notes." Maj. Gen. E. R. "Buck" Bedard and others felt that, for commanders, especially, if you didn't know your unit and know what you wanted to say, why were you in the job?

I think that rubbed off on observers, and in a good way. I witnessed many young company and battalion commanders "knock one out of the park," to say nothing of the colonels and general officers who continue to achieve promotion and success both in and outside the Marine Corps.

That said, frequent eye contact is more important than whether you use notes in most speech settings. And there's nothing wrong with injecting a reading that you want to deliver "exactly so"—perhaps a poem, a book passage, a letter or a specific policy statement from on high.

My personal preference is to memorize the outline only, not reading from, nor memorizing, a speech manuscript. By the time the event rolls around, my notes are reduced to that 3x5 card with maybe a half dozen outline bullets. I'll keep the card in my pocket or place it on the podium and, on a couple rare occasions, have had to very publicly refer to it during a speech. Not to worry. Research shows that audiences don't award credibility to a speaker who appears *too* glib or *too* perfect. If you're like me, you're golden!

While film clips and recruiting videos—and even PowerPoint presentations—have their place, I recommend being very judicious in their use. You may show up at a conference, for example, and decide that you don't want to use any "A/V" at all, after discovering that you're scheduled to speak right after lunch—and that the audience was briefed into a coma during a tedious morning session.

Finally, if you're to be bold in delivery—as you should be—stay humble and ever gracious in *attitude*.

You're wise to always remember that your appearance is "not about you." You are, in fact, representing somebody else: your command, your military occupational specialty, your alma mater, perhaps the commandant of the Marine Corps (officially, in some instances)—and everybody who has ever worn the uniform of a U.S. Marine. No pressure, right?

A few tactical considerations:

Arrive early. There's somebody else who is a lot more nervous than you might be—the person in charge of the program. You can be a tremendous blessing to him or her by arriving several minutes early, in addition to having stayed in close touch throughout the invitation process.

Speech-friendly bio. Provide your host a customized, brief introduction (both in advance and have one with you). If it can't fit on a 3x5 index card, it's too long. Typically-full-page (and longer) military "bios" are okay as program inserts, but they can kill an event's momentum when read verbatim from the podium.

Mix with the crowd beforehand. Even if the event is centered around a meal, it won't be inappropriate to visit a few tables and shake a few hands. You both win. People will deeply appreciate your approachability and accessibility, and you'll learn something important to perhaps add to your introductory remarks or elsewhere in your speech.

Eat sparingly before you speak. A full stomach will not help you be at your energetic best. Later, you can enjoy the satisfaction of a postevent cheeseburger in max-relax mode.

Slip a breath mint into your mouth afterward. This old preacher's trick is still a good one. Individuals will approach you to offer thanks for your address (or maybe invite you to speak at another event); you don't want to ruin the memory of a great Marine Corps oratory by knocking somebody back with your bad breath.

Avoid foul language. It doesn't matter who you might be quoting, or how wonderful that line sounds among your buddies—you risk offending your audience when you cuss. You may think you are building rapport with those Legionnaires, union machinists, or enlisted warriors—but you're actually disingenuously disrespecting them as a group (to say nothing of the individuals in the audience who teach Sunday School, possess graduate degrees, or otherwise fail to live up to your unfortunate stereotype of a particular audience).

Dump the podium. While some highly formal occasions may require that you be welded to the lectern, try to get out from behind that large, mahogany barrier, if you can. Studies have shown that the more of you the audience can see, the less you have to hide. Removing that perceived wall is a credibility enhancer. Be sure to ask what public address system limitations exist (and test the equipment, if you can). If you have a short-corded microphone attached to the podium, or a feedback problem because of the positioning of the speakers, you may be stuck. In that case, let 'em get a good, full look at you before (and after) you take your position behind the podium. (And the slight moving about can help you with that nervous energy you may be feeling.)

If the venue and audience are small enough, you may well be able to roam among your listeners (with or without a microphone), at least during the introduction and/or conclusion. This was practically a trademark for former commandant Gen. Al Gray. Remember: As speaker, you own the whole room, not just the stage. Use it! Picture yourself as a quarterback or, better, a commander with a wide view of the battlefield. Look the whole area over—and sometimes go there yourself. And when you saunter near one of the back corner tables, not only do the folks seated there appreciate it, so will everybody else. Such active engagement demonstrates that you are taking particular pains to be inclusive.

For Your Rucksack

An ancillary duty for a PAO or any community-minded commander is to energetically "adopt" your duty station and its immediate surroundings, stretching even to include your region and state. Become a visible cheerleader for your area! In so doing, you help to build a better city for your Marines and their families to live in; and you put feet on the "good neighbor" policy that the Marine Corps aspires to model in everything from social behavior to the environment.

Lutheran theologian Carl Bratten once said that "we cannot create unity, we can only recognize it." So it is with this thing called "community." All you have to do is publicly recognize and tout the genuine, practical symbiotic relationships that we sometimes take for granted.

If you're a post or station PAO, half your work's already done—by virtue of the civilian-military cooperation and partnerships that already exist in churches, Scouting, Little League, and the like.

Eddie Ellis, a business leader in Havelock, North Carolina, when I PAO'd at Cherry Point, was passionate about telling anybody who would listen what a truly cosmopolitan city we all lived in—because of the Marine presence. Eddie explained to his Chamber of Commerce colleagues (and to his newspaper readers) that their Navy-Marine neighbors came in from all over the country, often bringing a plethora of international experience, as well. Military members and their spouses were often alumni of some of the finest colleges and universities in the land, and more than anything else, they hit town with new ideas that could and should be thrown into the mix when making community decisions about school construction, roads, recycling, or how to get more people out for the Christmas parade or annual chili cook-off.

The Marines have certainly produced some great examples of the "adopt a community" mind-set. Maj. Gen. Cliff Stanley, now retired and heading a college education foundation, was so popular in the Town of Twentynine Palms, California, that they named the city park after him—while he was still there.

Maj. Gen. David Mize, whose calm and humble demeanor masked a legendary "why not?" approach to quality of life issues, started a charter school at New Orleans' Belle Chase Naval Air Station. And, at Camp Lejeune, he was pushing an on-base, phased retirement community situated in the woods next to the Naval hospital.

Community leaders loved General Mize's engagement, including golf foursomes every Saturday morning during which he made the rounds, literally, with key leaders of every stripe.

Chapter 5

SPECIAL OPPORTUNITIES

Exploiting Your Whole Toolkit

He who has a bountiful eye
will be blessed.

— PROVERBS 22:9 (RSV)

Besides the obvious public affairs duties you would expect to perform on a routine basis, special opportunities and resources abound. Your job is to recognize them and capitalize on them.

The Blue Angels

Most Americans have heard of the famed Blue Angels, the "stage name" for the U.S. Navy Flight Demonstration Team. But how many citizens, even Leathernecks, realize that, when they look up in the sky, there's a United States Marine at the controls of at least one of those lightning show ponies? Or a Marine crew manning the C-130 support aircraft, "Fat Albert"? Or Marine mechanics and logistics personnel who, along with their Navy counterparts, keep those F/A18 Hornets in fighting trim? Even a cursory surfing of the unit's Web site (www. blueangels.navy.mil) will give you photos and hometowns of more than a dozen Marines whose local and regional ties you can exploit next time the team performs in your area (or next time one of your captains or gunny sergeants—including those *formerly* stationed at your command—is named to that prestigious squadron).

Mine Those Bios

The Marine tradition of "team" over "individual" notwith-standing, it's a big deal when one of our fellow Leathernecks makes the cut and becomes a Blue Angel. Same with the Space Program, or being selected as a White House Fellow, or being tapped for brigadier general or sergeant major. A heads-up public affairs warrior will instinctively hunt down the biographical background on these standouts, often readily available as a one-page official bio. Again, you're looking for the local tie, the connection to your command. This is espe-cially true when the new commandant or sergeant major of the Marine Corps is named.

Another important billet not to be overlooked is that of color sergeant of the Marine Corps. The competitive post (Corpswide nominations are solicited via Marine Adminis-trative Message) is open to sergeants in all military occupa-tional specialties who meet the six-foot, four-inch minimum height requirement, along with requisite leadership skills and the ability to obtain a White House security clearance.

What about the color sergeant at your post, installa-tion, or major command? Or the aviator picked for test pilot school? Or the officer or enlisted Marine tapped for an over-seas exchange tour? Just doing our jobs? Maybe. But this is some pretty exciting, privileged stuff that we Marines are about—and our fellow citizens, especially "back home," deserve to know about it.

Toys for Tots

For those Marine Reserve units officially tasked with con-ducting a local Toys for Tots program, this is hard, sustained work—but it assures your organization of a welcome, unim-peachable presence in the community. Founded by the late Bill Hendricks, a Hollywood executive and Marine Reserve colonel, Toys for Tots has matured into a well-oiled machine, replete with top-level executive support and its own financial foundation, garnering significant corporate sponsorship. Done right—to include partnering with the entire local Marine family—Toys for Tots can generate an entire year's worth of good will in the few weeks the program is in the spotlight. (Those who work it, however, will tell you that the behind-scenes effort is almost year-round.)

The Silent Drill Team

Based at the historic Marine Barracks 8th and I in Washington, the twirling rifles and snap and pop exhibited by this ceremonial unit have wowed audiences worldwide. The savvy PAO will ensure that, when the Silent Drill Team comes to town, every local tie is exploited to the full. And your commander will want to host civilian dignitaries, treating them to a goosebumpy experience that'll put a lump in anybody's throat.

The Marine Drum and Bugle Corps

This is the musical group that travels with the Silent Drill Team; the two entities combine to give appreciative spectators the traditional, scripted Battle Color Ceremony. Is there an opportunity to host the entire high-school marching band in the stands? Or maybe have the drum major or one of the Marine musicians visit area schools? What about that trombone player or percussionist who is coming "back home" to perform in his home state?

The President's Own

Not to be confused with the Marine Drum and Bugle Corps or local command bands or D&Bs, the United States Marine Band is composed of some 160 members, specifically recruited to play at White House and other high visibility functions—including a national concert tour. Founded by an Act of Congress in 1798, "The President's Own" actually encompasses three musical units: the United States Marine Band, the Marine Chamber Orchestra, and various Marine Chamber Ensembles. Unlike other Marine Corps musicians, these performers do not have a secondary or tactical military occupational specialty. Members forgo formal "boot camp," in fact, and are enlisted at the rank of staff sergeant in deference to their formal musical training (often at the masters or doctorate level).

From a local public affairs perspective, your best opportunity is to leverage any local or regional stops on the band's annual national tour, (first authorized by President Benjamin Harrison at the behest of the group's most famous director, John Philip Sousa).

The Hollywood Marines

Every branch of service maintains a public affairs office in Los Angeles whose main purpose is effective liaison with the entertainment industry. You want this special Corps asset on speed dial. At some point during your tenure, the Los Angeles Marine Corps Public Affairs Office—the Hollywood Marines—are going to be looking for locations to shoot the next action-adventure film; or they need a young Marine of particular ethnicity to participate in a game show or special tinsel town event. Be the "go-to" guy for the L.A. office; it'll pay dividends for you and your command.

Sitting at my desk at Camp Lejeune one day, I got a call from ye olde Hollywood office—as I'd asked them to whenever they might need something. The Emmy Awards organizers wanted an enlisted service member from each of the services to do the famous "carpet walk" (and "live large" in L.A. for three or four days, including special dinners, tours, and parties) as honored guests of the Academy of Television Arts & Sciences.

As I recall, the only criteria was "a young corporal or sergeant" and that the lucky NCO be flown in from an overseas location. Too easy. I e-mailed my good buddy, Lt. Col. Willie

Jones, who was training his battalion in Japan as part of the six-month Unit Deployment Program (UDP). I explained the set-up and asked him to select one of his most deserving Marines for an all-expenses paid vacation back to CONUS. The entire evolution was a rousing success—and an ancillary benefit was giving recognition to our "forgotten battalion" on Okinawa.

Diversity

The Emmy event became a cause celeb for our shop, on at least two fronts. Twice a year, the Second Marine Division sent an infantry battalion and an artillery battery to East Asia, where, too often, they received but a fraction of the internal and external publicity rendered the warriors assigned to our wide-ranging Marine Expeditionary Units or MEUs (which enjoyed having their own six-man public affairs teams).

It was great to see those unheralded guys, half a world away, getting some quality time in the spotlight. We also deployed a staff combat correspondent to Okinawa for thirty days during our local Marines' training cycle. There's nothing like somebody showing up from home base—just to see (and write about) *you.*

But there's more to the Emmy Awards story: after inquiring as to the gender and race of the previously selected representatives from the other services, I ascertained that what was missing from the equation was an African-American male.

I thought, "Why waste an opportunity to also highlight the Corps' commitment to diversity?" It's a factor the PAO should always crank in; if you don't *think* about it and act, you end up with too many photographs, videos, and base newspaper front pages that simply fail to reflect the demographics of today's Corps.

Does your shop subscribe to *Ebony* and *Jet*? Do you provide tailored input (feature stories and photos) to those influential African-American publications? If not, why not?

Are you sending out any releases en español to the right outlets? If not, why not? When I instituted that practice at Headquarters Marine Corps some years back, one of my Marines wondered at the practicality, given that enlistees had to be English speakers.

True enough; but we weren't just after potential recruits—we wanted the parents and grandparents feeling good about their young person's interest in the United States Marines.

The New York City Office

Located in midtown Manhattan, the New York City Public Affairs Office is much like its sister operation in Los Angeles, except the Big Apple shop places special emphasis on the Corps' interests in the worlds of business and media.

New York has always been a Marine town, populated by a huge contingent of former and Reserve Marines who hold key posts in law enforcement, politics, the news media, and high finance. The city's robust, courageous response to 9/11 only solidified her partnership with the eagle, globe, and anchor.

When your boss is traveling to the Big Apple, the New York City Public Affairs Office can assist. They're also in the thick of it on events ranging from Fleet Week to the East Coast Media Training Symposium (an excellent opportunity for, especially, battalion and squadron commanders), to a Toys for Tots benefit Dining In that has been hailed as the ultimate night on the town. Liaison with the Intrepid Museum? Coordination with the Yankees or the Knicks? Best place to eat? In each case, and more, your answer man is the New York City PAO.

The Naval Academy

It's the Marine Corps' favorite enigma. Nestled on the banks of the Severn River in pretty Annapolis, Maryland, the U.S. Naval Academy is the college alma mater of fully one fourth of all Marine commandants. The "boat school" has also been the butt of jokes and the subject of much misunderstanding over the years, including the misguided notion that only graduates can teach there or that only children of alumni may attend.

In fact, the *Naval* Academy (never the *Navy* Academy) functions as "the University of the Navy-Marine Corps Team"—a 4,300-student college whose staff and faculty boast the largest Marine officer population outside the Corps mainstream (forty-three officers, seven enlisted).

Midshipmen are commissioned into the Navy or Marine Corps upon graduation ("we hire our graduates"), so those Leatherneck leaders assigned to "Canoe U" take very seriously their responsibility to award boat spaces to those with whom you and I will ultimately be serving.

No system is perfect—but since 1845, we've done pretty well in the inspiration department, whether it's producing bridge-blowing war heroes like the late Col. John Ripley, Class of 1962; or gridiron heroes like 2nd Lt. Zerbin Singleton, Class of 2008 and winner of Disney's Wide World of Sports Spirit Award, given annually to college football's most inspiring figure; or intellectual giants like former brigade commander retired Col. Art Athens, Class of 1978, the first Marine captain selected as a White House fellow.

Each year during my tenures at Cherry Point and Camp Lejeune, we did a big spread on the Naval Academy. As much fun as it was to point to John A. Lejeune or other legendary Marines, the real kick ("local, local, local"—remember?) was spotlighting the Leatherneck alumni on base, which always included senior colonels or general officers and hard-charging second lieutenants.

Why bother publicizing the Naval Academy? I can think of at least three reasons: (1) making our young enlisted Marines aware of the opportunity to attend via the Fleet Accessions Program, (2) making the teenage *children* of our middle-aged Marines aware of their opportunity to compete for a nomination and appointment, and (3) making all our Marines aware of the opportunity to serve at Annapolis in any number of fulfilling staff or faculty positions.

Taking Our History Seriously

If journalism is "the first draft of history," then certainly one of the PAO's inherent responsibilities is drafting the first draft of *Marine Corps* history. At the Headquarters level, the Division of History and Museums exists to support you. This energetic staff can help you research your unit's history, help you find that special photograph or painting, or assist you with that special project. This is likewise true of the National Museum of the Marine Corps.

Certainly the relationship with our historical running mates should be reciprocal, and the PAO is often the natural liaison when field historians or researchers or artists come calling at your base—or in the war zone. Help 'em out!

And don't forget to establish and maintain those critical relationships at the local level. You'll find that somebody has been assigned, or volunteered, to pay attention to command history where you are assigned; and *the librarian* is already your best friend, right?

Marine (and Other!) Affinity Groups

The Marine Corps Association. The Marine League. The American Legion. The Veterans of Foreign Wars of the United States (the VFW). The Marine Corps Aviation Association. The Military Officers Association of America. The Marine Corps Intelligence Association. That list, which could go on for miles, is a roster of your friends. These "affinity groups," many of whom have earned special status at Headquarters Marine Corps as members of the Marine Corps Council, are a magnificent local source for networking, a wonderful venue for your guest speakers, and a proven bench for volunteers.

They publish national magazines that often welcome stories and photographs from Marines; they boast well-tuned communications networks for getting your command messages out; and they offer many occasions for food, fun, and fellowship for Leathernecks and their families. Be sure to make 'em welcome: they can do you a lot of good and, more important, they represent a living link to the glories of our illustrious Corps.

Sports

From the Marine Corps Marathon to the U.S. Marine Corps Sports Hall of Fame, the eagle, globe, and anchor has been associated with athletics since before leather helmets. You'll find Marine Corps involvement at championship level in boxing, wrestling, archery, triathlons, rodeo, and motocross. We even sponsored a NASCAR entry for a time. It's more than fun and games, PAO. This is one more footlocker full of raw material that can be turned into community (and national) awareness and ready access to the publics we most want to reach.

For Your Rucksack

Harvest other media. I'm not talking about plagiarism, here. I mean get some bounce—some echo—from other media appearances by your people.

Example: Your command's got a major who pens an article for the *Marine Corps Gazette* or *Proceedings*. Or a corporal who snaps the cover photo for *Leatherneck*. Or a PFC who is the Marine featured on that *Leatherneck* cover. That's a big deal! Treat it as such. Seek permission to reprint that article or photograph, perhaps. At the very least, it's worth a "local Marine does good" mention in your command newspaper (and possibly in civilian outlets or the Marine's hometown). Obviously, you're already going to be using your own media outlets (Web site, base newspaper, command television, and any other means at your disposal) to cross-market. In other words, your Web site should point cyber surfers to your command newspaper—and readers to your Web site.

But be aware that there's a lot more available out there, if you'll only seek and ask. That's where your active relationships throughout the command and around the base will help you: You'll hear about the staff sergeant's wife featured in the *Girl Scouts Leader* magazine, of the chaplain profiled in *Catholic Digest,* or the corporal's video interview on television's *American Quarter Horse Journal.*

Exploiting success isn't just smart business: tactically speaking, it's the Marine Corps way!

Chapter 6

THE PROFESSIONALS

Some Warriors Do This for a Living

Last to know, first to go!
— MARINE COMBAT CORRESPONDENT
BOUND FOR KOREA, CIRCA 1950

A resourced, comprehensive effort to publicize Marine Corps activities did not come into being until 1941. An infantry officer and hero of World War I, Brig. Gen. Robert L. Denig, was brought out of retirement to serve as the Corps' first director of information.

Remembered today at "the Father of Public Affairs," his most well-known contribution was the raiding of America's newsrooms to recruit Marines. The innovative program saw seasoned writers, broadcasters, and photographers (some were as old as thirty-five) shipped out to boot camp at Parris Island or San Diego. Upon graduation, they were sent to Washington, D.C., for six months of orientation. ("Six months visiting our old watering holes, was more like it," quipped one of the original combat correspondents.) These new writer-fighters were then promoted to sergeant and deployed to the South Pacific, where they were folded into Marine Corps divisions and aircraft wings.

Typical was Claude R. "Red" Canup, a thirty-three-year-old sports editor in South Carolina who left home and hearth for recruit training and a lifetime's worth of adventure in World War II. Or Sam Stavisky, who penned his *New York Times* bestseller, *Combat Correspondent*, a full fifty years after his service throughout the theater. Or George McMillan, whose prolific postwar book writing included *The Old Breed.*

Modern-day Leathernecks charged with telling the Marine Corps story are accessed like most any other military occupational specialty. While the Corps occasionally recruits a journalism major or a school newspaper editor, most coming into the communication arts simply have a high enough test score on the Armed Services Vocational Aptitude Battery (ASVAB) and, hopefully, have a bent, if not a passion, for media-related work.

Happily, the information fields still manage to attract an interesting and talented bunch at all levels.

In 2008 Col. Katie Haddock retired at, arguably, the highest billet a Marine public affairs officer has held: she was PAO to the chairman of the Joint Chiefs of Staff, Gen. Pete Pace.

While the good colonel served in public affairs billets from the time she was a second lieutenant, the assigned leaders of the field—the directors of public affairs—have mostly been combat arms commanders pulling an obligatory staff tour at headquarters. Many of them brought their indispensible operational mind-set to the fight and, upon leaving the post, talked up the necessity of a strong public affairs program among their peers.

The most well-known example was probably Gen. Walt Boomer, who commanded Marine forces in Operation Desert Storm and retired as assistant commandant of the Marine Corps. Many attributed his media savvy and great relationship with the press to his brigadier general tour as the Corps' PAO.

The enlisted ranks have produced many a civilian newspaper editor, television producer, or public relations executive.

Tom Kerr, formerly at *USA Today*, comes to mind, as does *Leatherneck*'s Ron Keene, the late Clay Barrow at *Proceedings*, crack photographer Ernie Grafton at the *San Diego Union Tribune,* and Jim Kyser, well known in Washington's power corridors for the way he directed PR for the Association of American Railroads.

Then there's Dick Bugda, who started off as an infantryman, became a top-notch broadcaster and instructor, and transitioned back to line duties. The square-jawed Vietnam vet retired as a sergeant major a few years after taking a rifle company to Desert Shield/Desert Storm as first sergeant.

Or former SSgt. Jason Huffine, who deployed to Somalia and Iraqi Freedom and left an active duty career with a load of photojournalism awards to start his own newspaper. Today Jason is a public affairs officer in the civil service and has earned an enviable reputation for his groundbreaking work on such thorny issues as chemical weapons disposal.

The jack-of-all-trades title probably belongs to retired Maj. Bob Jordan. A former gunnery sergeant (he earned a Bronze Star, along with writing and photography awards, in Vietnam), Bob held most of the military occupational specialties taught at the Defense Information School. He's been an illustrator, photojournalist, broadcast station manager, and PAO—most notably for the 24th Marine Amphibious Unit in Beirut, Lebanon, when, on October 23, 1983, he had the heart-wrenching chore of handling public affairs duties in the aftermath of probably the greatest tragedy in modern Marine Corps history.

In retirement (probably a misnomer!), Jordan has been a business and marketing consultant, a *Leatherneck* writer, managing editor of *Homeland Defense Journal,* and coauthor (with Don Philpott) of *Terror: Is America Safe?*

At seventy-two, Bob currently serves on the faculty at Defense Information School and was a recent speaker at his other alma mater, Syracuse University, where, as a young gunny, he was the first broadcaster to complete the Military Photojournalism Program.

They're everywhere, these Marines who once pitched the Corps behind typewriters, cameras, and microphones. Pat Coulter, known as "The Voice of Raytheon," was a renowned broadcaster and PAO before carving out an enviable reputation in the corporate PR world, including honchoing the public communications for the famous Bell Atlantic-NYNEX merger.

Every American knows Jim Lehrer. Once the deputy public affairs officer at Parris Island, he's now an accomplished novelist, anchor for PBS' *Lehrer News Hour*, and, perhaps most famously, the moderator for a series of presidential debates.

Seen any good war movies lately? If you did, chances are that retired Marine PAO Capt. Dale Dye had a hand in them—and likely appeared in them as well. Regarded in Hollywood as *the* outfit that trains actors how to be soldiers, Dye's Warriors, Inc., has helped shape such blockbusters as *Saving Private Ryan, Platoon*, and *Forrest Gump*.

The sometimes controversial, oft-misunderstood Al Jazeera Arab news network boasts a former Marine combat correspondent and public affairs officer on staff: Josh Rushing, who was prominently featured in the film, *Control Room*.

Same with Jon Stewart's *The Daily Show*. Reserve major and comic Rob Riggle has earned a faithful fan following as a roving reporter on the satirical news program. At this writing, Rob was in negotiations with CBS to develop his own starring vehicle.

Not that being a PAO is all fun and games. He jokes about it now, but during the Tet offensive in 1968, 1st Lt. Jim DiBernardo became, in his words, "the only Marine to lose a TV station in combat." He spent five years in North Vietnamese prison camps.

Those charged with telling our story have made the ultimate sacrifice, as well, including those engaged in Operations Enduring Freedom and Iraqi Freedom.

In 2004 Cpl. William Salazar was killed in Afghanistan, followed two years later by PAO Maj. Megan McClung's death in Ramadi.

Maj. Trane McCloud, a battalion operations officer who once headed Navy-Marine Corps News, died in a helicopter crash-landing on Iraq's Lake Qadisiyah the same week Major McClung was killed.

Several Marine storytellers have been awarded Purple Hearts during what Marine commandant Gen. Jim Conway has called this "Long War." Perhaps best known is Cpl. Aaron Mankin, severely burned during Operation Matador in Fallujah in May 2005, when the tracked vehicle in which he was riding rolled over an improvised explosive device (IED).

The Rogers, Arkansas, native has been an articulate and inspiring spokesman for his fellow warriors, having had his continuing story of gutsy rehabilitation chronicled in dozens of media venues, including lengthy features on CNN, ABC, MSNBC and in *Best Life* magazine.

Defense Information School

The Defense Information School, known for many years by its syllabic acronym, DINFOS, is the U.S. government's only resident school for public affairs and visual communicators. Youngsters right out of boot camp receive college credit for intense, almost "immersion," training in videography, still photography, print and broadcast journalism, public affairs, and related disciplines.

Alumni are later eligible to attend an array of advanced courses that run the gamut from military newspaper editing to broadcast station management. And, in the school's Public Affairs Leadership Department, a renewed emphasis on follow-on opportunities has birthed a series of "graduate-level" courses that the most senior public affairs professionals can attend.

Unique in the U.S. Armed Forces, DINFOS is an officer and enlisted training home to every branch of service—including the Coast Guard—and regularly welcomes interagency students and those from dozens of foreign nations.

A Matter of Association

A not-so-secret weapon for Marines assigned as public affairs or audiovisual professionals is the U.S. Marine Corps Combat Correspondents Association (USMCCCA), formed during World War II by those first "CC's." The Association serves up professional seminars at an annual conference, which is highlighted by the presentation of "Best of Corps" media awards—representing nearly fifty categories—at a formal banquet. But the most valuable benefit of membership is the advice and networking available to those assigned to today's information fight.

My introduction to some truly seasoned hands came during *Exercise Alkali Canyon* at Twentynine Palms, California, in the summer of 1973. Some nine thousand Marines, half active duty and half reservists, were flown in for the maneuvers, and our Command Information Bureau reflected a 50/50 active/Reserve mix, as well.

And what a wonderful mix it was! Our director was Col. Jeremiah "Jerry" O'Leary, one of the original Denig's Demons and a veteran Washington reporter in civilian life. He had the White House beat in his latter years, attending those presidential press conferences for the old *Washington Star* and, later, the *Washington Times*.

The other reservists had similar resumes, including the travel editor for the *Los Angeles Herald-Examiner* and a sportswriter for the *Cleveland Plain-Dealer*. Just to be in the same "newsroom" with these ink-stained (and combat-tested) characters was a real kick in the pants, especially for a nineteen-year-old lance corporal who, just a year earlier, was writing sports for his small hometown weekly.

And the active duty types, many not long returned from Vietnam and mostly officers who tended to be predominantly mustangers (former enlisted), were pretty interesting to be around, as well.

By affiliating with the Marine Corps Combat Correspondents Association, the expertise, example, and tall tales of the lot of them were readily available to me for the span of what was to be a thirty-year career.

Two specific examples come to mind:

As the PAO at Marine Corps Air Station, Cherry Point, North Carolina, in the late 1980s, it was my duty to handle the media interest attendant to my first aircraft mishap (aviators hated that word "crash"). Before I walked down the passageway to discuss the matter with the Second Marine Aircraft Wing commanding general, I called retired Lt. Col. Jack Lewis, USMCR, and read my draft news release over the telephone.

"Uncle Jack" had many years with "the Wing" in war and in peace, and it had been my pleasure to serve under him at a later stint at Twentynine Palms. He was, and is, a Marine Corps public affairs legend, authoring some thirty books as a civilian author and publishing a bevy of magazines (including *Horse* and *Horseman*, *Gun World*, and *Bow and Arrow Hunting*) as president and publisher of Gallant Charger Publications.

The former rodeo cowboy dispensed with a word or two of wisdom, suggested a couple of tweaks to the release, and voila!, the young captain is pitching an intelligent, well-researched product to his approving commander.

About seventeen years later, I got a Saturday night call from the staff secretary of the Second Marine Expeditionary Force, letting me know that the chief of staff and I were to meet Sunday morning with the commanding general concerning an Osprey crash in Arizona. Again, I did not go in empty handed, providing my boss with both a draft news release and a draft condolence statement. I was a lieutenant colonel by then, but Marine Corps training had taught me you're never too old or too seasoned to have somebody check your work—so it was with the CG's blessing that I shot a copy out to La Jolla, California, where retired Maj. Bob "Mo" Morrisey was living.

Mo had been the special assistant for public affairs to the commandant in his twilight tour and launched immediately into a successful civilian PR career in the aerospace industry. Both qualifications were helpful to us, because the Osprey was still very much a technological work in progress and political interest in Washington was at a peak. It would be another seven years, in fact, before the tilt-rotor aircraft would join the fleet. Putting out a factual, contextualized release was important.

Again, it was through the USMCCCA that I came to know Mo, and we enjoyed a wonderful, twenty-year friendship up until his death in 2005. Not content with leaving his mark in both Marine Corps and civilian PR (he and his late wife, Mary Jane, whom everybody called "M. J.," were especially involved in the Apollo 13 program and knew and supported all the astronauts and their wives), Mo started a trendy California-based newsletter on the subject of wine. More than 2.6 million readers know his publication today as *The Wine Spectator*.

Is there any doubt that a young (or older) PAO would have something to learn from a Jack Lewis or a Bob Morrisey?

For Your Rucksack

If you're a commander, give your PAO top cover. Whether he or she is full-time or collateral duty, he has the best chance to thrive and prosper on your behalf if you make it clear to him and to the entire organization that you are personally involved and committed to publicly telling your unit's story.

Nobody's asking you to coddle him. But he will likely be among the most junior people on your staff, and you are tasking your PAO with plying a trade whose seeming simplicity can be quite deceptive.

Including her in meetings and planning sessions early will pay huge dividends for all concerned. Ditto on direct access to you, including regular one-on-one sessions. She needs to know where you're coming from if she's going to communicate your vision throughout and beyond the command. The PAO is your communications counselor, the special staff officer who will prep you for media interviews, lock on speaking gigs (and write or provide input to those speeches), and, if you like, ghostwrite your letters to the editor and lengthier thought pieces for both internal and external publics. Hard to do if you don't have the old man's ear.

And if you're the public affairs officer, there are a few important things you need to do in order to earn your commander's robust support. More on that in chapter 9.

Chapter 7

SHINY NEW TOYS

Information Age Hardware and Concepts

It's clever, but is it art?

— RUDYARD KIPLING

Shortly after American forces charged into Baghdad in the spring of 2003, the concept of an "information war"—particularly the sense that we were on the losing end—began to capture attention. But five years later, resources had not even come close to matching interest in this "new" art.

Case in point: the user-driven YouTube video craze and its electronic cousin, MySpace, were popular with a large segment of (especially) young Americans many months before military officialdom took notice. The bureaucracy's first reaction? To ban both from government computers. About a year later, the U.S. Army had introduced TroopTube and all the Services had actually joined forces with MySpace—just about the time a widespread security ban was placed on both photo cards and memory stick devices in all Defense Department computers.

So our institutional relationship with the so-called new media has been halting at times—but not without resounding success in some areas. If you're the guy or gal tasked with getting out the word on your organization, you certainly want to be aware of what's out there and, to the greatest extent possible, to use the new toys to their fullest advantage.

Before looking at some of the avant-garde tools and paradigms, two words of warning are in order:

1. Don't fall in love with the technology for technology's sake. Case in point: Ever watch a bad television show or

surf through an error-laden, difficult-to-navigate Web site? As with kinetic weapons systems (or even a whole new realm of arms—for example, aviation), the new information tools will never approach their full potential unless effective tactics are developed and practiced for their use.

2. Don't forget what got us here. In the case of public information, especially public information destined for consumption by American audiences, that means not jettisoning some classic, time-tested principles that have everything to do with servicing independent news media—and being straight up with the taxpayers who loan their sons and daughters and give their treasure to the Marine Corps.

While we've progressed from physically transporting media pouches across the battlefield on a regular basis, the need to do it the old-fashioned way still exists—at least as a backup.

Tools of the Trade

Given the necessary lead time in getting a book to market, the terms "at this writing" or "as we go to press" are most appropriate. It won't be very long before the "new media" becomes the "old media." Whatever toys we're using now will be, no doubt, upgraded to enhanced, newer versions or even replaced altogether during the course of the next couple of years.

Or as Marine colleague Lt. Col. Riccoh Player put it to me: "This chapter will be dated no matter when it is published."

Regardless, those with public affairs responsibilities better be pretty nimble with the ever-emerging technology. Universal computer expertise seems to have replaced horseback riding skills as a given for all officers—and the PAO needs to be able to produce and transmit media-quality imagery, as well (while never being caught without pad and pencil in his flack jacket pocket, just in case).

The World Wide Web (Revisited)

Everybody's got a Web site, but the old adage applies: in for a penny, stay for a dollar. Those who rely on the World Wide Web for their information have demonstrated an insatiable appetite for real-time data. Regular, if not constant, refreshment is key—being sure not to sacrifice speed for accuracy. Fact-checking, grammar, and spelling still count. For PAO work, perhaps the Web site's highest value is its function as an electronic bulletin board. You can get the results of the court martial or investigation and "hang them on the Web," even automatically alerting your news media via e-mail that the goods are now available. Sure beats two hours spent on the telephone with a call list and a clipboard.

Blogs

Same rules apply. Easy to start, but hard to maintain. Does the commander do a blog? Does somebody write it for him, or does he do it himself? How many people are actually reading it? Is the investment of time and energy worth it? How much time and effort can you afford to monitor (other) blogs that comment on your activities or are otherwise tied in to your mission? As with polling, perhaps somebody else can do the detail work for you—at a price. But will their deliverables be accurate? Can they give you the information age version of "actionable intelligence?"

Social Networking

Here's a phenomenon that has taken off—but how do you manage it? You can stay connected with your high school or college classmates, your fellow Marines, fellow public relations professionals, your MySpace friends, the virtual working group you belong to tackle that special project, your Naval War College study group—the list goes on. For those adroit enough to juggle all the passwords and move easily from one account to the next, maybe more is better. And, as mentioned in the chapter introduction, the military services are getting on board. With some apparent success, recruiters are trying to harness the craze as an aid to win hearts and minds—especially hearts and minds in the eighteen-to-twenty-four-year-old range.

Twittering

A cousin to the BlackBerry, twittering has become the darling of the must-stay-connected types—but its potential and efficient use can go beyond superfluous "tweets." Imagine, for example, needing to communicate a schedule change to a dozen different media reps who were en route to your position. A couple of clicks on your iPhone, and the chore is done.

Telephone Menus

"Pay close attention, because our options have changed." Sound familiar? When speed matters, as it usually does in this business, those phone menus can drive you crazy. Make sure your particular system does not add to the electronic traffic jam that characterizes our workaday world.

Digital Photography

A boon to tactical commanders, major news organizations, and grandparents everywhere, digital photography has long since come of age. Its speed and clarity, in both still and video form, have revolutionized the photography industry. Less than a generation ago, well-traveled war correspondents had to develop photos from cobbled-together field darkrooms, often relying on carrier pigeon methods to get their prize-winning shots back to the rear.

Cell Phones

Mobile communication has become required; but like e-mail, its use can become obsessive. As long as you pay due attention to security and safety (avoid talking while driving, please), this is a convenience that has more than proved its worth. Common courtesy seems to have taken a hit, however. There was a time when it was considered rude to take a telephone call in your office when you had a visitor; with today's "virtual office," some people don't even treat themselves (or their guests) to an uninterrupted lunch. Have you noticed, too, that 10 percent that have never gotten the word on silencing their cell phones in a meeting or lecture?

DVIDS

Otherwise known as the "Digital Video and Imagery Distribution System," DVIDS has been one of the major success stories during this current span of wartime deployments. Billing themselves as a state-of-the-art, 24/7 operation that "provides a timely, accurate and reliable connection between the media around the world and the military (serving overseas)," DVIDS warriors make available on-line some 3,600 publications as well as nearly 115,000 broadcast-quality video and news products and 133,000 still images.

The Defense Department entity coordinates fast-breaking news interviews with commanders and subject matter experts in the field; it enables embedded civilian journalists to transmit from remote locations; and it facilitates the standard "holiday greetings" and live sports and other special events programming that used to take days to coordinate (and sometimes for a tape-delay presentation, at that).

The Manual Typewriter

Just kidding.

Having trouble adjusting to all the gadgetry and cyber forums? Don't feel alone: When the U.S. Naval Institute (USNI) announced its launch into the blogosphere in December 2008, a blogger named "Chap" saw the need to issue a "Fogey Alert" on the site: "This is a good time to abuse the privilege and get something straight, just to keep people from looking like they just came from the Lawrence Welk concert. Okay, look here, senior people, you guys with the VCRs at home flashing '12:00.' The whole website here, that thing you clicked on to get here? That's a *blog*. This article-looking passage? That's a *post*. Anybody writing little blurbs after the post is written? Those are *comments*. Don't be like that guy, please."

It's not just old warriors going through some growing pains. Sometimes the technology bites back. The same month that USNI began blogging, network anchor Brian Williams introduced with some fanfare a live "PuppyCam" on the NBC *Nightly News*.

People all over the world viewed the Internet with fascination, he said, as a litter of puppies jumped and played and ate and cuddled. Now, between major stories on presidential cabinet appointments and an economy that was in the tank, Williams cued the live shot, so all America could ogle the pups via television, the original global village.

Neat idea. Except the puppies were almost entirely off camera, huddled in a corner of their kennel. And fast asleep.

Stakeholders

As revolutionary as some of the shiny new toys may appear, even more crockery is being broken in terms of structure, organization, and philosophy as the defense establishment wrestles with proper roles and definitions across the wide information battlefield. Besides the PAO, entities to be considered include, but are not limited to:

Information Operations

Aimed at the bad guys, information operations is about integrating electronic warfare, computer network operations, military deception, and psychological operations. The key is to protect ours—and disrupt his—by getting inside the enemy's automated (and human) decision-making mechanism. In 1947 Congress forbade Service public affairs organizations from getting in the "influence" business; as you might hope and expect, influence is "job one" for the IO wizards, along with their mission to "disrupt, corrupt, and usurp."

Psychological Operations

"PSYOP" seeks to alter behavior of foreign populations in a manner consistent with U.S. diplomatic, national security, and foreign policy objectives. Activities might include leaflet drops that encourage enemy soldiers to surrender, or native-language newspapers and broadcast aimed at "winning hearts and minds." Loudspeakers are still used in a variety of ways (including blaring the song, "I Fought the Law and the Law Won," when Manuel Noriega was holed-up in Panama City's Papal Nuncio during Operation Just Cause in 1989). A key point in U.S. law: Psychological operations can never target—and that's the verb that is used—our fellow countrymen.

Civil Affairs

Commonly seen overseas coordinating engineering work, food distribution, or school support, civil affairs specialists render the deeds that back up America's words when war or famine strikes.

Activities performed or supported by civil affairs (1) enhance the relationship between military forces and civil authorities in areas where military forces are present; and (2) involve application of civil affairs functional specialty skills, in areas normally the responsibility of civil government, to enhance conduct of civil-military operations.

Combat Camera

Clearly operational in its focus (more on that in the next chapter), combat camera delivers battlefield still and motion imagery in support of strategic, operational, and tactical mission objectives. DoD Instruction 5040.4 notes that "Combat Camera imagery may be used as a secondary intelligence resource," but its chief mission is to acquire imagery in support of "the operational and planning requirements of the National Command Authority, the Chairman of the Joint Chiefs of Staff, the Military Departments and the Unified Combatant Commands."

Detailed requirements for combat camera include battle-field and mission assessment, situational awareness, and legal documentation.

Strategic Communications

Ahhhh, the paradigm du jour.

As defined in DoD's *Dictionary of Military and Associated Terms* (Joint Publication 1-02), strategic communications are "focused U.S. government efforts to understand and engage key audiences to create, strengthen, or preserve conditions favorable for the advancement of U.S. government interests . . . through the use of coordinated programs, themes, messages and products synchronized with the *actions* of *all instruments of national power*." (italics mine)

Can there even *be* a director of strategic communications at less than the national level? Would the information czar at, say, U.S. Central Command, be more properly cast as a director of *operational* communications?

We went through the same growing pains when terms like "joint" and "combined" came on the scene. We've been increasingly "joint service" since at least the Normandy Invasion—but in 1988 I reported to Cherry Point as director of joint public affairs, with nary a soldier, sailor, or airman in sight.

Job title aside, it might seem that a military director of strategic communications would have all command information assets under his or her leadership. But even that part continues to be worked out in many major commands and among the Services, especially where the public affairs piece is concerned. Stay tuned.

The Commander

Here's the *real* stakeholder, the tiebreaker, the one who sees himself as being personally and directly responsible to the American people for mission success. In 2008 major U.S. commands in both Iraq and Afghanistan were still perfecting their structure vis-à-vis getting the word out to each of their disparate audiences, including their own troops, the local populace and its leaders, the enemy, our coalition partners, folks back home, national and international news media, higher headquarters, and the Congress.

In King Leonidas' day, a mental matrix probably helped him manage his information customers; today's warrior-leaders practically require a spreadsheet and a graduate-level staff to interpret it.

The particular challenge to an *American* commander is that our citizens don't take kindly to disinformation, misinformation, half-truths, sugar-coating, or "spin." Recent efforts that have even *hinted* at a coordinated, comprehensive, targeted propagandistic approach have been met with swift and sure repudiation.

In 1917 Senator Hiram Johnson forever ensconced himself in journalism culture with his statement, "The first casualty when war comes, is truth." Our job, your job, is to be keenly aware of that well-deserved cynicism on the part of your countrymen—and to combat it with DINFOS commandant, Navy captain Curry Graham's, coin(s) of the realm: "Truth, trust and credibility."

For Your Rucksack

Clearly, with the vaunted twenty-four-hour news cycle (which isn't a "cycle," at all—it is *continuous*), we are saturated with information.

"There is no real 'beginning' or 'end,'" Defense public affairs guru Bob Hastings has said. "So the PAO can rarely achieve finite mission success in the classic sense."

Or as Cpl. Matt Killion used to say at Cherry Point, "we're always blowin' and goin.'" And generally you're not in "practice" or exercise mode, either. Whether in peace or war, those are *real* news conferences, interviews, speeches, and all the rest.

After six chapters of describing the lush, plentiful targets that populate the PAO's world, let me now talk out of the other side of my mouth: Relax. Take a break. Have balance in your life.

If family, health, and taking care of your troops hold any significance to you at all, you must regularly and forcibly step away from the sensory overload and recharge your batteries. Make it a priority.

I like the take offered by *Full Frontal PR* (Bloomberg Press, 2003) authors Richard Laermer and Michael Prichinello: "Speed is good in sports and fabulous in microwaves. When we begin to hurry through life, however, things get ugly. Many of the most important things in the world take time and thought! When we sacrifice that, we lose in the end, and there's nothing touchy-feely about the result. Slow down and contemplate. Your ability to create brilliant, imaginative PR—not to mention a host of other things—will only benefit."

Even God took a day off.

Chapter 8

STILL WORTH 1,000 WORDS

Every Picture Tells a Story

The soul cannot think without a picture.

— ARISTOTLE

S peaking at the U.S. Marine Corps Combat Correspondents Association's National Conference in San Diego in 1985, now-senator Jim Webb (D-Va.), the Marine Vietnam War hero then serving as the Reagan administration's assistant secretary of defense for reserve affairs, told of a friendly exchange in his office. A colleague from the Army, noting a poster-sized, framed photo of a grunt in Vietnam, asked Webb how he could tell whether the warrior was a soldier or a Marine.

After all, the snuffy in the picture wore the same helmet and the same torn, sweat-soaked camouflaged uniform and carried the same M-14 as any dogface or Leatherneck tromping through the jungle.

"Isn't it obvious?" asked Webb, a twinkle in his eye. "It's gotta be a Marine—there was a photographer there!"

Much of what we've talked about in this book explicitly, or at least implicitly, identifies the importance of imagery in telling the Marine Corps story. But the pictures, not just the words, are important enough, even critically important enough, to merit their own chapter.

To the greatest extent possible, a sharp PAO always offers the media an image, or an image opportunity. He's going to be asked for one, anyway!

Even if you are launching a simple news release about a new command policy or an aircraft mishap, provide a photo of the commander in the case of the former and a stock photo (and fact sheet) in the case of the latter. The media are going to be looking for these items from the Internet or from their own file photos—and what they use may not be what you consider the "right" image.

Case in point: At Camp Lejeune in the very hot summer of 1999, the Second Marine Expeditionary Force (II MEF) suffered an inordinate number of heat casualties. We called a local, well-attended Friday afternoon news conference to get words of concern and stated policy straight from the horse's mouth—the commanding general, Maj. Gen. E. R. "Buck" Bedard.

The front-page story in Saturday's *Jacksonville* (North Carolina) *Daily News* was certainly accurate in its reportage, but how much more appropriate it would have been if I'd thought to furnish a photo of the commander with his "war face" on. As it was, the *Daily News* reached in their files for their first shot available, a broadly smiling two-star Marine general under a headline that spoke of death and danger.

Not just photographically speaking, but in every area of mass communications, the prize goes to the PAO who makes it easy for the editor. An over-the-top customer service approach (without sinking into blatant self-promotion or pandering) wins the day—every time.

A Marine Corps Staple

The most famous photograph of all time? There is, has been, little argument worldwide. The shot still seen 'round the world is the late Associated Press photographer Joe Rosenthal's image of five Marines and a Navy corpsman raising the second, larger flag on Mount Suribachi on the island of Iwo Jima on February 23, 1945.

Countless magazine articles and at least two books have been devoted just to that photograph alone. The photo later gave birth to a statue; and Felix de Weldon's massive creation (each man depicted is ten meters tall) is situated in Arlington overlooking our country's capital.

A short distance south in Quantico, the National Museum of the Marine Corps—with its contemporary, easily recognizable, angled steel pole—seems to almost subliminally echo the Iwo flag raising as it draws in motorists from Interstate 95.

Such has been the impact of *that* shot. That iconic moment atop Suribachi is bigger than our Corps; it has become a symbol of our nation—and, indeed, a symbol of perhaps our nation's most precious ideal and her most treasured export: freedom.

Another recent example of the photo's powerful effect was the History Channel's documentary on combat camera training. Keying off actor/director Clint Eastwood's tandem World War II cinematic success in *Flags of Our Fathers* and *Letters from Iwo Jima,* the History Channel crew, like Eastwood, was enamored of the idea that an image could evoke such heartfelt passion—and action—including enlistments, war bond contributions, and untold deeds of bravery since.

The History Channel peeled the onion further by focusing on the training received by military photographers and videographers at the Defense Information School at Fort Meade, Maryland, knowing that the pictures these youngsters capture can yet today have a huge impact.

A combat motion-picture version of the original event was filmed by Sgt. William H. Genaust and was a newsreel and television sign-off staple for years. It was also featured in the John Wayne classic, *The Sands of Iwo Jima.* Sergeant Genaust was killed in fighting just a few days later.

Will we see another photograph like Rosenthal's? That would be a tall order. But in battles since, the photographs of David Douglas Duncan, Horst Faas, Eddie Adams, Steve Stibbens, Larry Burrows, and countless others have captured the essence of the Marine.

Perhaps no shooter has painted that essence so well lately as Lucian Read. His color shot of bloodied, pistol-wielding

1st Sgt. Brad Kasal being helped by his men from a bombed-out building in Fallujah was determination personified.

That image of now sergeant Major Kasal has not inspired a statue (yet), but it has so far given us at least one book cover, a limited-edition poster produced by the Marine Corps Association at the behest of Gen. Jim "Mad Dog" Mattis, and the *Marine Corps Times* cover story that first propelled the Navy Cross recipient's heroics into the spotlight.

For active duty Marines in the picture biz, the mother of all spotlights shone on Tarawa more than sixty-five years ago. Not only was the fighting there among the heaviest—and most legendary—of World War II, it also was the most well documented, as well. SSgt. Norm Hatch, "armed" with a 35-mm Bell & Howell Eyemo motion-picture camera, told *Naval History* editor Fred Shultz that it was "the only time, to the best of my knowledge in both the Pacific and European Theaters, that a cameraman was fortunate enough to capture both sides in a fighting stance."

What Hatch was modestly referring to was his unprecedented, extraordinary footage of Americans and Japanese killing each other amid the fury of a desperate battle—one that found him in the thick of it. President Franklin Roosevelt himself cleared the footage for public release, and in 1944 *With the Marines at Tarawa* won an Oscar for short-subject documentary, and SSgt. Norm Hatch's name was on the marquee in Los Angeles when the film debuted.

Norm Hatch, now eighty-eight, retired as a major and today remains extremely active in the International Combat Camera Association, the U.S. Marine Corps Combat Correspondents Association and as editor emeritus of *Follow Me*, the monthly newsletter of the Second Marine Division.

Some Marine combat motion-picture cameramen gave their all. In 1967 Sgt. William T. Perkins was on a patrol during Operation Medina in Vietnam when the unit he was documenting came under attack. During the firefight, an enemy grenade rolled next to Perkins and his fellow Marines.

The nineteen-year-old unhesitatingly covered the explosive with his own body, dying in the blast. Perkins was awarded the Medal of Honor. In memory of his service and sacrifice, the William T. Perkins Combat Videographer of the Year is named each fall at the U.S. Marine Corps Combat Correspondents Association Awards Banquet.

Structure and Organization

As this book goes to press, both the Marine Corps and the Army are wrestling with how best to organize and deploy those warriors whose expertise is strictly in the visual communications realm, including combat camera. For the Air Force and Navy, the decision has already been made. Since about 2006, the writers, broadcasters, photographers, videographers, and PAOs have migrated to a common boss (director, communications and public affairs for the Air Force and chief of information for the Navy, which also unveiled a new, consolidated rating: mass communications specialist).

Do all our "shooters" and "pencils" have to share the same box on the org chart, so long as they are joined at the hip in a de facto sense, when and where our communicators' dual expertise is critical?

I asked then-Maj. Gen. Marty Berndt to put us under the same umbrella at the Second Marine Expeditionary Force at Camp Lejeune in 2001—but he did not see the necessity.

"As long as you have a solid working relationship," he told me. "They don't need to come under the PAO. You can still get the job done."

And he was right. In fact, his commonsense response, honed by years of combined arms, joint, and international experience (he was the commander whose unit rescued downed Air Force pilot Scott O'Grady in 1995), is some of the best, practical advice any PAO could have. Your success at telling your unit's story is always contingent on the cooperation of people and organizations that you do not "own."

As a lieutenant, I thought it rather tedious that I could not do something as simple as publish a brochure without engaging the print shop, a graphics artist, the photo lab, and perhaps other agencies outside my official scope. But hindsight has shown me that this is the stuff of which relationships are made. The traditional preference—the pipe dream, really—of having all your needed experts physically at your fingertips has gone the way of the buffalo.

Seeing things from the combat camera's viewfinder helps. Just as you need a clear understanding of civilian media demands, your work in promoting your command requires you to understand the visual communicator's bailiwick. (And, as is the case with Joe Civilian Reporter, you'll often be the picture-taker's advocate.)

The key point to remember is that a combat cameraman's raison d'être is as an operational photographer or videographer. He or she is engaged in critical missions that can have life or death ramifications, including beach surveys for amphibious landings and other reconnaissance and training priorities (to say nothing of a vast catalog of "how-to" videos for the Corps increasingly multitasked "strategic corporal").

While the PAO has responsibility for seeing how the organization is perceived publicly (think of the television broadcast of an NFL game), combat camera is in charge of the "game film," capturing angles and priorities for the coach's (read: operational commander's) purposes. Although it's wonderful when an audiovisual product can serve both the operator and the PAO—understand that, in case of a tie, the operator wins. (More accurately, the *commander* wins. And there are certainly those times when *el heffe* sees the need to make combat camera, or the lawyer, or even a subordinate commander, defer to PAO's recommendation for the greater good.)

A special frustration for particularly your videographer and broadcast brethren is the misinformed notion pushed by some seniors as to how quickly products can be turned around. Just because it takes two minutes to watch it, that doesn't mean it took two minutes to produce it! In fact, the standard industry ratio for broadcast-quality work is one-minute air time equals one-hour production time.

Photographer's Best Friend

And what can you bring to the table on combat camera's behalf? If you're any kind of a PAO at all, you represent solid relationships—with the community, with the command, with the media. And you can share that largesse with your brothers and sisters who labor behind the lens. Your photographer outreach program might include:

Highlighting Their Work

While PAOing at both Cherry Point and Camp Lejeune, we worked with the officer in charge of the combat camera unit to recognize his Marines' fine work. We set aside an entire page of the command newspaper each quarter to showcase a single photographer's images. I didn't care whether they were military shots or not; this was a chance for a young Marine to show off his talents. And we always included a photo and thumbnail bio of the photographer himself.

Promoting Photo Contests

With combat camera's focus (no pun intended) on operational support, they're just not as attuned to media opportunities (including some great photo contests) as the PAO is. That is a big part of his job, after all. So, share the wealth! Make it a habit to always reach out to your picture-snapping brethren to let them know about some dandy contests, with sometimes huge cash prizes, conducted by the U.S. Naval Institute (www.usni.org) and others. You can also use your retail exchange manager and Chamber of Commerce contacts to come up with some pretty decent prizes for your own photo contest. And routinely encourage photographers to grab that cover shot—for any publication. And when they succeed, shout it from the rooftops. *Leatherneck*, the "Magazine of the Marines," particularly does this well. Each of the twelve covers in a given year is decoupaged on a handsome wood plaque and presented to the respective photographer. Then, the editors choose the best cover of the year and render the Tom Bartlett Award (and a sizable check).

Unexpected Professional Courtesies

When a photographer within your scope of influence grabs a great shot of the commandant or commanding general or other VIP, it's a pretty simple matter to make arrangements to get a copy made and personally signed by "the big man" to give to the "photog." Your lensman will appreciate the gesture for a long, long time. And if he does a particularly striking job in a publication over which you have some control or influence, get that photospread mounted or framed (and always encourage your photojournalists to start or maintain a portfolio of their work).

Tactical Tips

Giants of the Corps

One morning in 1990, Col. Mike Hayes was referring to an old, back-pages *Leatherneck* feature when he gathered his staff for a "Giants of the Corps" picture on the roof of the warehouse that served as headquarters for Marine Forces Panama. With the Bridge of the Americas clearly depicted in the background, we all had a nifty souvenir of an exciting and effective operational deployment. We may not have had Butler, Lejeune, and Puller in the photo—but these were our fellow Marines, and I've no doubt that a framed 8x10 is displayed in more than one den or study (no doubt alongside a promotion or reenlistment photograph or two—personal milestones for which a caring commanding officer ensured documentation). For my money, the minimal time and coordination required to set up shots similar to ye olde "team picture" is energy well invested.

Now, there are purists out there who don't think the PAO should be involved in morale-boosting efforts like "Giants of the Corps," much less unit T-shirts and who knows what else (Army Lt. Col. Bob Donnelly told me that "PA" stands for "practically anything"). To them I would ask: exactly whom did you have in mind?

More in the next chapter on unique ways you can *contribute* to the team, rather than shy away from natural opportunities that drop in your lap.

Candids, Candids Everywhere

When a new commandant takes office, or a new commanding general, or a new sergeant major, there will be a standard, head-and-shoulders studio photograph made available for distribution for posting at subordinate-level headquarters, commissaries, Marine Corps Exchanges, and the other usual places where "the man" can be easily recognized.

But you can go one better. Whenever the new CMC came calling at a base where I was stationed, we would brief-up the photographers to shoot all the film they needed to capture a decent *candid* shot. If you really nail it (perhaps a particular turn of the head or thoughtful expression or animated gesture), that photograph can take on a life of its own, giving Corpswide base newspaper editors (and others) a refreshingly different view of the new top Marine. And it's nice public recognition for the shooter whose work, if it's good enough, may well be seen all over the globe.

On the local level, I'd send my photographers with a shot list that would include not just the regimental commanders who were changing command, for instance, but some of the familiar luminaries who were sure to be in attendance (chief of staff, commanding general, sergeant major). That way we'd have some good, nonposed photos "in the can" for those later occasions when one of our local leaders would be retiring or chosen for a new rank or billet.

Regardless of your shot list, you want never simply to send a photographer sans instructions. Brief him up. Tell him what you need. And whomever you've put it charge—be he or she writer, broadcaster, or photographer—have them boldly introduce themselves to the senior Marine present. That's the opportunity to let the on-scene commander know who you are, what you're shooting, and, importantly, to ask if the boss has any other requirements or requests.

In an ideal world, all these details have been worked out at the staff noncommissioned officer level; but it's no secret that the fast-moving world in which we operate is far from ideal. And there's this guy named Murphy who has a tendency to show up when you least expect him.

Publicity Stills

Candid shots notwithstanding, those head-and-shoulder shots can come in pretty handy—and so can an effective throwback: the publicity still. Whether snapped in a studio ("crafted" is probably a better verb) or at a remote location, a solid, posed photo pays for itself in both utility and longevity. Picture a Marine all geared up in his flight suit or field kit, showing his best war face. They're great for calendars and base guides, in-house ads for the command newspaper, "commercials" for the base TV station, and Marine Corps Birthday Ball programs and other commemorative materials.

Those aforementioned head-and-shoulder shots? Perfection would mean having one available on every Marine in the unit. At a minimum, you need to have in hand the mug shot of every commander and sergeant major down to the battalion level, and, in the case of a deploying Marine Expeditionary Unit, every company and detachment commander, as well. Many heads-up MEU public affairs officers will leverage their technology (read "digital photography") and organizational relationships to gather photos on everybody in that two-thousand-man lash-up. Even during times of relative peace, this is

highly trained all-star team (literally certified as "special operations capable") designed and dispatched to patrol the trouble
spots of the world. The statistical likelihood is high that the
MEU and the warriors in it will be doing something histori-
cally significant. Kudos to the PAO who is ready to respond
with words *and pictures.* Research tells us that the human eye
is naturally drawn to the human face; a photograph of the CO
provides a newspaper (or a television station) a nice "graphic"
to break up the words in a piece and, more important, gives
the reader or viewer something to focus on (especially com-
pared to the other articles and stories which were *not* deliv-
ered "with art").

Combat Art

A particular area where the Marine Corps "gets it" is in the
realm of old-fashioned paint and easel art. Despite the cut-and-
paste convenience of computers, despite the computer-assisted
weakening of the MOS, and despite the rapid advance of other
media, the permanence of oil paintings, charcoal drawings,
even sculpture has survived.

They're called "manual arts," and if your command has
somebody skilled in them, don't ignore their impact.

Those armed with paintbrush, charcoal, drawing pencil, or even wire loop sculpting tools can bring permanence
to history than even the best writing and photography has
difficulty matching. The PAO can exploit the intrinsic value
of the artist's work by arranging for and publicizing exhib-
its on base and "out in town" and by reproducing paintings,
sketches, and cartoons in the command newspaper. He'll also
want to release digital images of Marines' artwork to civilian
media; Marine Corps drawings and paintings are in the public
domain, same as a good photograph.

Posters, brochures, displays on the headquarters quarter-
deck—all are richly enhanced by the efforts of what Defense

Information School art instructors wryly refer to as "combat crayon."

CWO2 Michael D. Fay, one of only two officially designated combat artists in the Corps, told the *Marine Corps Times'* Jason Watkins that there is "something ineffable" about old-fashioned paintings and drawings.

"You really can't put it into words," Fay stressed. "That's why imagery exists."

Commandants since the Corps' earliest days have recognized the power of art enough to approve dozens of individual excursions, sometimes using retired or contracted artists, to more permanently document not only operations and exercises worldwide, but humanitarian missions, as well.

How important is combat art to the fabric of the Corps? As the 22nd Marine Expeditionary Unit prepared to float in late 2008, the CO, Col. Gareth Brandl, thought it fitting that a contingent visit legendary Marine Corps artist Charles Waterhouse during a gallery exhibit at New York City's Salmagundi Art Club.

"Walk around here and (these paintings) will speak to you," said Waterhouse, a retired colonel and the only person to have been posted as resident artist of the United States Marine Corps.

Calling the display "history that will be remembered forever," one of Brandl's charges, military police officer Cpl. Tara M. Emerick, was about to sail into harm's way with two thousand of her most intimate friends. Or more, if you count those who went before her: legions of Marine warriors never to be forgotten, thanks to the Corps' unshakeable link to the past.

Whether it's traditional canvas art, still photography, or pictures that move, the PAO is seriously underarmed and absent an understanding—and aggressive application—of the power of visual media. My teaching colleague, Navy Lt. Cmdr. Jon Spiers is spot on when he insists that his public affairs leadership students grasp "Spiers' Big Three": resources, marketing, and imagery.

For Your Rucksack

Try never to allow a photograph to be published absent a photo credit—and that means the shooter's *name*, not just "Official Marine Corps Photo." And while that certainly goes for printed matter over which you have control, such as base newspapers, base guides, and calendars, you should leverage your influence and relationships with other media, as well. You'll, of course, provide full credit information when releasing imagery to media outlets, but on those occasions where credit goes missing (or it's only generic credit), let the editor know! A phone call or e-mail should do it; and sometimes a letter to the editor is even better. The photographer's name makes it into print, and everybody concerned sees that photo credit is important to your command.

That simple, courteous act will speak volumes about putting people first—and appreciating their contributions.

THE GLOBE

Serving Camp Lejeune and surrounding areas since 1944

VOLUME 71 EDITION 1 | WWW.CAMPLEJEUNEGLOBE.COM | THURSDAY JANUARY 8, 2009

UBAYDI, IRAQ

Tank Marines work hard, stay on track

CPL. SEAN P. CUMMINS
Regimental Combat Team 5

Heaving heavy tanks over miles of rough terrain means the tankers and tank mechanics in western Anbar province, Iraq, have their work cut out for them when it comes to keeping their vehicles running.

The Marines of 3rd platoon, Co. A, 2nd Tank Battalion, have been operating out of Combat Outpost Ubaydi, supporting combined antiarmor teams from Weapons Co., Task Force 3rd Battalion, 7th Marine Regiment, Regimental Combat Team 5, as they patrol near the Syrian border.

"Mainly, we do overwatch and security for the infantry as they go out to the border forts. A lot of times we support each other, but now since there is no armor threat, we're trying to find different ways to employ tanks while we're out here," said Gunnery Sgt. Jeffrey T. Peeler, a platoon sergeant with 3rd plt. "We provide that security for them to make sure they're safe while they do their job."

To make sure everything is running right, the Marines of Co. A, work around the clock, inspecting every piece of track and greasing every lube point whenever they have the chance.

"The primary focus is to keep these tanks up That way they can go out and operate, make sure they get the job done," said Sgt. John L. Green, maintenance chief with 3rd plt. "Every day there's something going on with these tanks. My

guys are always working weird hours. The tanks go down at random times."

Every morning the Marines head out to their M-1 Abrams main battle tanks to begin daily maintenance: checking fluids, looking for loose bolts and cleaning off censors.

"We work on the tanks every day. Every hour of operation is about eight hours worth of maintenance, so daily they're out here running the engines, hitting all the grease points, hitting up every hole point, and making sure our weapons are good to go," said Peeler.

While on missions the tankers themselves must be prepared for anything. Anything from hydraulic systems and hub seals to tracks and transmissions can break at any time.

"One task threw track and we had to break it and put it back on," said Lance Cpl. Andy A. Goldsmith, a gunner with 2nd Tank Bn.

Upon return to base, the tank crew must perform after-operations maintenance so they are ready for the next day.

"(After-operations maintenance) consists of walking the track and making sure none of the track is lose or coming apart and then checking all the suspension components, drive components, final drive components, checking for leaks, stuff like that," said Sgt. Ryan S. Wilson, a tank commander with 3rd Plt.

"The guys that haven't been out here before aren't used to troubleshooting different problems with the suspension because that stuff doesn't go down at Camp Lejeune," said Green. "It's a more rocky climate (in Iraq); the heat changes the performance of the hydraulics and you just have to learn to adapt. They're just trying to get used to different conditions, so there is always something new that they're learning."

Photo by Cpl. Sean P. Cummins
Cpl. Steven D. Bowling, a 21-year-old tank mechanic with Co. A, 2nd Tank Battalion, Regimental Combat Team 5, rigs the crane of a M88 Hercules to the power pack of an M1A1 tank and signals for it to be pulled out Dec. 29.

Photo by Cpl. Sean P. Cummins
Lance Cpl. Marc J. Revis, driver, Co. A, 2nd Tank Battalion, Regimental Combat Team 5, pulls a chain of .50 caliber rounds from a can to inspect them for rust or broken links that could cause a jam while firing Dec. 28.

MARINE CORPS BASE QUANTICO, VA.

Three-time war veteran passes away Monday

QUANTICO SENTRY
Marine Corps Base
Quantico

Veteran of three wars and author, Lt. Gen. Victor H. "Brute" Krulak, 93, died Monday in Southern California.

Krulak, served with distinction through World War II, Korea and Vietnam. He

later penned "First to Fight: An Inside Look at the Marine Corps," which remains today on the Commandant's Reading List.

Born Jan. 7, 1913, Krulak began his distinguished career began upon graduation from the U.S. Naval Academy in 1934.

As a lieutenant colonel in the fall of 1943, he

earned the Navy Cross and the Purple Heart on Choiseul Island, where his battalion staged a week-long diversionary raid to cover the Bougainville Invasion. Later, he joined the newly formed 6th Marine Division and took part in the Okinawa campaign and the surrender of Japanese forces in the China area. There he

earned the Legion of Merit with Combat V and the Bronze Star.

After the war, he returned to the United States and served as assistant director of the Senior School at Quantico, and, later, as regimental commander of the 5th Marines at Camp Pendleton. He was serving as assistant chief of Staff,

G-3, Fleet Marine Force, Pacific, when the Korean Conflict erupted, and subsequently served in Korea as chief of staff, 1st Marine Division, earning a second Legion of Merit with Combat V and Air Medal.

In July 1956, he was promoted to brigadier general and designated assistant commander, 3rd Marine

Division on Okinawa. From 1957 to 1959, he served as director, Marine Corps Educational Center, Quantico. He was promoted to major general in November 1959, and the following month assumed command of the Marine Corps Recruit Depot San Diego.

SEE VETERAN 7A ▶

Lt. Gen. Victor H. Krulak

LOS ANGELES

'Scars are not forever'

Medical innovations bring hope to disfigured hero

STAFF SGT. ETHAN E. ROCKE
Headquarters Marine Corps

It was an ideal. A mantra. One of those romantic assertions that grabs hold the heart and crams in the soul the question: What if?

"Scars are not forever," was conceived for one Marine in the months of rehabilitation that followed an IED blast in Iraq, which left him badly burned and disfigured. Since then, the spirit of that ideal has evolved into an innovative partnership between military and civilian medicine that is actualizing, for some, that once rhetorical question: What if?

Aaron Mankin lay still on an operating table, bright halo-

gen bulbs spilling light over every bit of his fair-skinned face: closed eyes placid with unconsciousness, relaxed jaw peeking out from the feature between rich, disfigured lip tissue, an incision on the right side of his nose stretching the length of it.

The ordered bustle of the operating room lay outside, for above the anesthesia.

There, Dr. Timothy Miller, chief of reconstructive and plastic surgery at the University of California, Los Angeles Medical Center, looks down at Mankin's face and focuses.

Coolly marking Mankin's face with a pen outline, Miller had described the goals of the procedure, Mankin acknowl-

edging with a characteristic smile and nod - a gesture of enduring trust in that man whose scalpel has been to Mankin's face what da Vinci's brush was to his Mona Lisa.

"I take your pictures home with me, ya know?" Miller said during the examination, referring to the dozens of photographs he uses to track the evolution of Mankin's face before and after operating on it a dozen times.

Mankin reached to his throat to close the airway of his tracheotomy and push the air from his lungs up through his damaged vocal chords.

"Oh yeah?" he said, his

Photo by Staff Sgt. Ethan E. Rocke
A skin graft taken from Aaron Mankin's chest is placed over the exposed tissue left on the left side of his nose after doctors performed a surgery Nov. 18 at UCLA Medical Center. Mankin has had more than 50 surgeries since he was wounded May 11, 2005.

soft, raspy voice contrasting smiling, wide eyes.

This is Mankin's twelfth surgery under Miller's hands - "magic hands," say some of the coworkers and patients. The lofty, soothing melody of Frank Sinatra's "Fly Me to the

Moon" wafts in the operating room as Miller makes a precise and gentle sawing motion with his tiny scalpel, a handful of doctors and nurses looking on. He trims away unnecessary

SEE SCARS 7A ▶

BLT 3/2 RAID COURSE
PAGE 4A

The traditional internal information source has been the base newspaper. (Camp Lejeune *Globe* image courtesy Ena Bravo, Landmark Military Newspapers of North Carolina)

The formal Washington news conference, here featuring Maj. Gen. Marty Berndt, remains a mainstay of public affairs. (Defense Department photo by R. D. Ward)

First Lt. James Jarvis conducts a field expedient press conference at Kandahar Airport not long after Marines began operations in Afghanistan in 2002. (*Marine Corps Times* photo by Rob Curtis; reprinted with permission)

Toys for Tots, initiated by Marine Reserve Col. Bill Hendricks in 1947, has linked the Corps with America's favorite holiday ever since. (Photo by Dean Dixon, courtesy Marine Toys for Tots Foundation)

Maj. Nathan M. Miller is but the latest Leatherneck to be part of the famed Blue Angels, a superb but sometimes underexploited Marine public affairs opportunity. (Photo courtesy U.S. Naval Flight Demonstration Team)

Maj. Gen. Charles Bolden, the current NASA administrator, is one of a long line of well-known Marine Corps spacemen, going back to John Glenn. (NASA)

The classic "publicity still" has not outlived its utility. In this 1951 shot, Navy Corpsman Dan Heath of Walnut Cove, North Carolina, prepares to leave for Korea. (Photo by Donald O. Graw)

Cpl. Scott Wyatt won a combat art award in 2008 for his color pencil drawing that paid homage to Navy Cross recipient Sgt. Maj. Brad Kasal. (Image courtesy USMC Combat Correspondents Association)

National Museum of the Marine Corps

Triangle, Virginia

It's no accident that the National Museum of the Marine Corps harkens visitors and passersby to the most iconic moment in Leatherneck history. (Poster reprinted courtesy Gwenn Adams and the National Museum of the Marine Corps)

Maj. Megan McClung, post-humously promoted, was the first Marine public affairs officer killed in Operation Iraqi Freedom. (Courtesy Michael McClung)

"Passing the torch" remains an important tradition of Marine Corps public affairs. Current PAO Capt. Al Eskalis enjoyed a National Press Club dinner in 2005 with three of his tribal elders (l–r): Norm Hatch, Cyril O'Brien, and Sam Stavisky. (Photo by John Metelsky)

Typically Marine in historic approach is former *Leatherneck* artist Chuck Beveridge's design incorporating Mt. Surabachi with a contemporary image from the Iraq theater. (World War II photo by Lou Lowery; Operation Iraqi Freedom photo by Cpl. Graham Paulsgrove)

The "Betio Bastards" of 3rd Battalion, 2d Marines, in action in Iraq. (USMC photo by Cpl. Ray Lewis).

Maj. Pat Coulter, a public affairs officer of some renown, built a successful career in corporate and aerospace public relations after retiring from the Corps. (Photo by Pfc. Shejal Pulivarti)

Lt. Col. Riccoh Player was feted by no less than Secretary of Defense Donald Rumsfeld and DoD's top PAO, Torie Clarke, on his last overseas flight in support of Pentagon press operations. (Photo by Helen Stikkel)

The U.S. Naval Academy has produced many a Marine, including 2007 football star and brigade commander Zerbin Singleton. (Photo by MC2 Thomas Gilligan)

Drum Major MSgt. Kevin Buckles naturally commands attention when he leads the famed United States Marine Corps Drum and Bugle Corps. (Photo by Sgt. John J. Parry)

"Results. No Alibis."
-- Maj. Robert B. "Mo" Morrisey

In remembrance of one of the great ones, from the Provisional Maryland Chapter, USMCCCA at Defense Information School, Ft. Meade, Md.

Jason Fischer, Chapter President.

www.robcookdesign.com

The late Maj. Bob "Mo" Morrisey, who was special assistant for public affairs to 23rd commandant Gen. Wallace M. Greene Jr. when he retired, cut a wide swath in both the military and civilian worlds of PR and journalism. (Sgt. Rob Cook design courtesy USMC Combat Correspondents Association)

Medal of Honor recipient William T. Perkins is remembered annually by a special award that bears his name. (Sculpture by Donnie Shearer; photo courtesy USMC Combat Correspondents Association)

Chapter 9

FOR PAOs ONLY

Surviving and Thriving in a Niche Role

> Noah didn't wait for his ship to come in—he built a boat.
>
> — AUTHOR UNKNOWN

When I first began to seriously read and study public affairs and public relations in the mid-1970s, I discovered a palpable, cultural inferiority complex among professionals, in both the military and civilian sectors.

Folks in this biz often did not have the proverbial "seat at the table" when important, strategic decisions were being made; they were "last hired and first fired," promotion opportunities (and pay) were slow in coming, and their relative worth was difficult to measure (if any measurement apparatus even existed).

It seemed every edition of the *Public Relations Journal* included a required woe-is-us article.

In the military, Public Affairs was too often a "safe" place to stow an officer passed over for promotion. Or, noted Fred Woodress in *Public Relations for Community/Junior Colleges*, "maybe a misfit dean or losing football coach gets the nod from the president who has no idea that public relations is really a profession."

Vestiges remain today.

But the good news is that the landscape has changed. PAOs are now expected to be at "the grown-up table" (as Torie Clarke likes to say). And thanks to recent, high-visibility leaders like Gen. David Petraeus, Gen. Anthony Zinni, and others, America's future admirals and generals are observing—and applying—the reality that public affairs is important to their commands because gaining and maintaining public support for their policies is absolutely necessary for those policies to succeed.

What to Do?

Despite (or maybe because of) some institutional improvements, the onus is still on the individual to prove his value to the command—every day.

My 2003 *Marine Corps Gazette* piece, "Back to the Future in Public Affairs" (appendix 1 in the back of this book), referred to "Ten Extras to Ensure Public Affairs Success." I penned that list in 1995, and those simple points were validated for me a few years later when I was serving as a voting member of the Marine Corps Lieutenant Colonel Selection Board. In reviewing the records to help choose the Corps' next generation of senior leaders, it became obvious to me that— when my colonel peers and I examined the personnel files of "specialists," for example, those serving in Public Affairs, Disbursing, Law, Data Processing, and so forth—there were two kinds of Marine officers: operators and nonoperators.

By "operator," I don't mean a full-time assignment or transfer to tanks or attack helicopters. I'm talking about a warrior, team-player *mind-set*. The fitness reports written on the promotion bound reflected a career characterized by energy and enthusiasm in the things that really matter to a Marine, including taking care of the troops, staying in top physical shape, marching to the sound of the guns, and taking seriously pop-up executive officer assignments or even collateral duties that can run the gamut from armory inventory to having a key role in a command ceremony or VIP visit.

Here's an annotated version of "the list":

1. Be a Marine first. The privilege, and responsibility, of being a Marine Corps public affairs officer is that you aren't just a spokesman for the Marines—you *are*

a Marine. And you've got to *be* a Marine, first. Only then do you concentrate on being a Marine *officer* and, finally, with those first two roles articulated clearly in your heart and mind, do you pay due diligence to your performance as a Marine PAO.

2. Study other PR/media organizations. Remember that choosing which media to consume (and *when* and *how*) remains one of the most personal acts enjoyed by our fellow citizens—even those in uniform. So you might be wise not to limit yourself to "military" tactics, techniques, and procedures. Think you can learn something from *USA Today*, the NFL, MTV, or Warner Brothers pictures? From *Rolling Stone, Thrasher*, the video game industry?

When I stop for gas on a road trip, I'm the guy who forks over a tax-deductible buck or so to grab the daily (and weekly) newspaper(s) available in the locale I'm driving through. I'll usually spend all of five or ten minutes on each publication, gleaning tips I might employ in terms of layout, design, and content, and I get a heartland view of how the Marine Corps (and other services) are being presented and perceived among our citizenry.

Another habit I've cultivated over the years is to get my public affairs shop on the mailing lists for major college football programs and Hollywood studios (a simple letter requesting some is all it takes). We circulated throughout the office the sports information guides and movie press kits we received to give our folks the opportunity to see how other industries do our job. As a bonus, the base newspaper editor had early, studio-quality scoop and images to publicize the motion pictures when a film made it to the base theater. And sometimes embedded in the materials was a Marine connection we could harvest for a story: the former enlisted defensive back, the Vietnam veterans assistant coach, or the former Marine actor. Besides, receiving those colorful, splashy materials was good for morale. Everybody had a chance to peruse product from "my team" or movie (and sometimes "call dibs" on a poster or set of publicity stills on a favorite star).

3. Join the USMC Combat Correspondents Association. By now, you've probably picked up on my passion for *associating* (if not, please see appendix 4). By joining a professional association, particularly this one, you expose yourself to the benefits of mentorship, networking, and giving back. In the case of the USMCCCA, you're signing on with an especially unique, exclusive outfit. Thirty-five years later, I still can't get over the fact that I continue to be helped along by fellow Marines of all ages who have been generous with their time and their very specific, immediately applicable experience and counsel.

4. Think comprehensively. Take a "combined arms approach" to your duties. Leverage your three-pronged public affairs attack by always integrating your community relations and information functions.

5. Keep your antennae up. Have a "bountiful eye" out for Marine tie-ins and application of trends and issues. If you've got your thinking cap on, you won't go to a movie or the mall or even thumb through a magazine in the doctor's waiting room without being hit broadside with a neat idea or two.

6. Participate in the "extracurriculars." The old saying that "a lot of business gets down on the golf course" is as true as it ever was. And you don't want to neglect the other de facto meeting rooms, like the running trail, the weight room and sauna, and the officers' club. Colleague Mike Gannon, a retired senior Air Force public affairs officer, used to have the job of flying from Washington to inspect his service's PAOs. He always insisted on lunch at the Officers' Club, he said, because he could quickly

gauge how "plugged-in" the local PAO was, from the interactions he observed (or not!).

7. Kill the "I don't have time" monster. You will not have time to do absolutely everything; get over it. But the more passes attempted = the more passes completed.

Cultivating the habits described in items 5 and 6 will go a long way to aiding you in your crusade to lead the most effective public affairs shop in the Corps.

And here's another tip: join a civic club. Whether it's Rotary, Kiwanis, Civitan, or another reputable group, you'll be getting into what I described to my wife as "grown up Boy Scouts"—people who meet weekly, usually at breakfast or luncheon, for the stated purpose of serving the community. Does some networking take place? Does some business get done? Does some good scoop get passed? You betcha. Which is why it's worth your time and money (tax deductible dues for you, PAO) to keep you and the command "in the loop." You'll also be leaned on to help recruit guest speakers and to solidify relationships between the citizenry and their military (which reflects your job description rather nicely!).

The late Navy captain "Ned" Beach, after whom the Naval Institute headquarters is named (along with his father, Capt. Edward L. Beach Sr.), was kind enough to help us jettison our excuses by writing books on active duty, including his famous tribute to the submarine service, *Run Silent, Run Deep.* How did he manage it? According to Edward P. Stafford's preface, Beach wrote his award-winning novel "early in the morning, on weekends, on leave, and in whatever spare time was left to an officer serving as naval aide to the president of the United States."

You won't have enough *people* on your staff to do absolutely everything, either. Working with your Reserve Liaison Office, you have the ability to recruit and maintain some sharp reservists, and their rank or military occupational specialties are not necessarily critical.

Solicit volunteer columnists, television program hosts, even people who'll be willing to help you answer the phones. Gym rats and rock groupies are not the only people who like to hang around a particular activity (and be involved, if they can). Find those news junkies who enjoy the pace at a TV studio or a happening public affairs shop, especially when things are hopping because of a big deployment or perhaps a high-visibility court martial. More than once hard-working Marine spouse volunteers were able to beef up their resumes with us—and then go on to paying jobs with area media.

8. Practice people skills. When I was assigned to the faculty of the U.S. Naval Academy in the mid-1980s, the late Col. John Ripley was the Marine Corps representative and director of the Division of English and History. The Navy Cross recipient called the Marine staff together for a meeting before the academic year began and shared his philosophy (and our guidance) for dealing with midshipmen. "I want you always to model 'The Three A's,'" he said. "Be *approachable*, *available,* and *accessible*."

   Don't ever play the Grand Pooh-Bah. *You* be the one to initiate relationships, place the phone call, make the visit. Be a proper host when folks come calling, whether it's a reporter, the president of the enlisted wives club, or a community leader. Offer coffee, listen, and pay attention to their concerns. Be aware that you'll never succeed alone. There's a reason why Marines embrace the concept of esprit de corps—French for the biblical expression, "spirit of the *body*."

9. Read! Reading is obviously a big part of your job, but to be successful, you've got to go well beyond your basic requirement to stay informed via the daily newspaper and the *Early Bird,* the Defense Department's compilation of national security related stories. You'll keep on

top of current Marine Corps thinking by subscribing to the *Marine Corps Gazette* and you'll get a wider view by reading the Naval Institute's *Proceedings*.

Nowadays, you've no doubt added Web "surfing" to your intellectual weaponry, as well. A special favorite for me, though, is a good book. For one thing, it forces you to slow down a bit—an aspect that's just as important to your overall health as proper diet and exercise. The PAO should be familiar with such military classics as *Once an Eagle*, *We Were Soldiers Once . . . and Young*, and *The Caine Mutiny*.

You'll gain great leadership insight from tomes like these, as well as from more contemporary "how I did it" stories from the likes of Navy captain D. Michael Abrashoff (*It's Your Ship: Management Techniques from the Best Damn Ship in the Navy*, Business Plus, 2002). But don't get all your books from the military shelf. Again, Laermer and Prichinello in *Full Frontal PR*: "One of the coolest things about being a really informed person is that you'll be brimming with fresh ideas, from fashion to corporate management. You then become one of those sources reporters love: A PR pro who tosses out interesting ideas and trends, even if they're not always linked to a story about your company of product."

10. Don't wait for the rocker (or bars, or stars). By "rocker," I don't mean the one on your front porch (but don't wait for *that* one, either!). I'm talking about the uniform insignia that promotes a young sergeant to the middle management ranks as a staff noncommissioned officer. As is the case with marksmanship, physical fitness, public speaking, and other "individually graded" activities, many aspects of public affairs do not genuflect at the altar of seniority. Passion is passion; excellence is excellence.

Retired Maj. Gen. Cliff Stanley, who directed Marine Corps Public Affairs in the late 1990s and commanded the

Corps' vast Mojave Desert training base at Twentynine Palms, California, had some great expressions. One of my favorites was, "There's no such thing as 'justa'" (as in "just a staff sergeant" or "just a lieutenant").

And another Stanleyism was close to it: "Rank doesn't have a thing to do with it." That statement addresses not only looking beyond your relatively junior standing to achieve spectacular team or personal results; it's also about the positive influence you can have, the meaningful encouragement you can give, to those around you—including your boss.

Out and About

An infantry colonel told a PAO buddy of mine, "if you're sitting behind your desk, you're not doing your job." The requirement—and the fun—of getting "out and about" should be a given.

When I arrived for duty at Cherry Point to direct both Air Station and Wing public affairs as a captain, one of my most enjoyable activities was to visit the various units (where some COs told me I was the first PAO ever to darken their door).

My first week on the job, I went out to the rifle range with my Master Guns and my "Mickey Mouse ears" (hearing protection) and the range officer remarked that "it was good to see a commander come out; we don't host that many COs anymore." Probably beaming, I let the gunner know that I was not a commander, but his comment reinforced my heartfelt belief that getting out from behind the desk creates a good vibe for all concerned. The visit set a positive tone for working with my new senior enlisted adviser, as well. Most important, that simple act of basic Marine Corps leadership made a good and lasting impression on Sgt. Cheryl Silge, the Marine we were coming to see.

I had learned the goodness of going to see my folks from a former PAO boss (who also happened to be a very good shot): now-retired Lt. Col. Jim "The Freckled Flash" Vance.

Two years later, we were in the thick of moving thousands of Marines to Operation Desert Shield/Desert Storm when

I needed to make another kind of visit. Cpl. John Raughter had wrecked his motorcycle delivering a news release to area media. On my way out the door, my new noncommissioned officer in charge asked, "Skipper, are you sure you should be going the hospital just now?" He knew we were prepping for a major news conference and other deadline-driven events tied to the operation.

"Yeah, Top, I'm sure," I told him. "Especially now. Sends a good message."

Postscript: John Raughter healed up, made sergeant, and got out of the Corps to pursue college. He eventually earned a master's degree in journalism and became editor of *American Legion,* the largest-circulation magazine on the planet.

Years later at Camp Lejeune, I'd expanded on the "out and about" theme, posting some of my lieutenants all over that far-ranging base. One had full PAO responsibility for all the tenants of Stone Bay, which included the rifle range and the Special Operations Training Group; another went to work every day at Camps Johnson and Geiger, where he paid special attention to our infantry and logistics training; a third created a morale-boosting information fiefdom at Courthouse Bay, providing public affairs support to the amtrac battalion and the engineer school.

We learned that it takes a Marine colonel about five minutes to get used to the idea of having his own PAO—and that's exactly what we wanted to see happen. This was especially beneficial for our "CAX Det" program, in which we deployed a lieutenant and small public affairs-combat camera team to California's Mojave Desert in support of the Marine Expeditionary Force's twice-yearly combined arms exercise.

Here you had a regimental commander leading live-fire maneuvers for five thousand Marines during a six-week period, employing virtually everything in the Corps' arsenal, including jet aircraft. Injecting public affairs into the war games enhanced training (and relationship building) for all concerned; the PAO brought practical help to the fore when the CO had to deal with a training accident or another real-world incident.

And for the first time, all those Marines from Camp Lejeune weren't "out of sight, out of mind." The PAO regularly dispatched stories and images back to North Carolina (and elsewhere) and even arranged for home-based civilian news media to catch a hop to the desert on more than one occasion.

Get a Mentor

Perhaps the best resource of all is the acquisition of a mentor—especially a Marine public affairs mentor born with a Ka-Bar in his teeth and black newspaper ink running through his veins. The good news is, they're out there. If you're going in cold, the best place to start is to contact the national headquarters of the U.S. Marine Combat Correspondents Association (www.usmccca.org).

When I served as senior Marine at the Defense Information School in the mid-1990s, one of the tasks I gave each fledgling Leatherneck PAO during "Service-unique" training was to engage one of our field's area "tribal elders." Students pulled a name from the hat the first week of the eight-week Basic Public Affairs Officer Course. They were to turn in a brief written paper by course's end, based on their interview with somebody in the Washington-Baltimore area who had "been there, done that." The program was a rousing success: the lieutenants' eyes and historical consciousness were alert to the gold mine of experience available to them; and the mostly retired PAOs and staff noncommissioned officers seemed to genuinely appreciate being asked to participate. And a couple of the more enterprising and forward-thinking officer students worked to keep the mutually beneficial relationship going long after graduation.

Point is, "mentoring" is alive and well. Reach out!

Can't find a mentor who fits the "exact" description? Improvise! Whether you're in Phoenix, Cleveland, or Charlotte, you'll be able to find somebody who will willingly give of his or her time to help you succeed in your public affairs chores. He or she may not be a Marine at all. Many former and retired PAOs from other services are happy to lend a hand as often will a military-friendly retired journalist or public relations executive.

For Your Rucksack

Your goal can't be to get promoted. That'll come—or not. The key is to get so involved in doing the right thing—and, again, making it fun—that promotions and awards, if you are so blessed, are just a natural by-product.

What you *do* have to be mindful of is the degree of influence and access that may, at first, surprise you. Not your *personal* influence, mind you, but that which comes with the office of public affairs leader. Your presence, even if you're junior in age or rank, can be extraordinary throughout the community and command. A case in point is the position of the Marine Corps Recruiting Command's "MPAs"—the marketing and public affairs representatives.

Often young sergeants in their early twenties, MPAs are generally posted far from the flagpole in major American metropolitan areas. Their one-man job is to be the public affairs presence for the hand picked Marine major charged with recruiting that region's youths into our beloved Corps. The responsibility can be pretty heady, and the best MPAs practically "own" the city to which they're assigned, having built positive relationships in the mayor's office, at the Chamber of Commerce, and, certainly, among a plethora of media outlets.

Similarly, a good PAO shoots, moves, and communicates in some pretty fast company; he or she is the commanding general's principal source for timely, accurate information on both the command and the adjacent civilian communities.

Even as a junior officer, and even if you only stay in the Corps for a single tour, it can and *should* be an invigorating ride.

Chapter 10

OUTTAKES AND BLOOPERS

Nobody's "Perfekt"

Some of the best lessons we ever learn, we learn from
our mistakes and failures. The error of the past is the
wisdom and success of the future.

— Tryon Edwards

Did I always get it right? Goodness gracious, no! In fact,
documented below are a few boneheaded public affairs
moves I've made over the years—so you won't have to.
Those with whom I've served could, no doubt, cite dozens
(if not hundreds) more times when I squibbed it, but I shall
appeal to their graciousness—and on behalf of many defense-
less trees—in setting some artificial limits.

Don't let 'em rush you. The scene was the Havelock High School
football stadium where the Marine Corps Battle Color Ceremony contingent was conducting its second area performance
of the day. We did it off base to send a message of neighborli-
ness and solidarity with the community surrounding Marine
Corps Air Station Cherry Point. So far, so good.

But for whatever reason, the mayor did not show for the
event and the 8th and I coordinator was looking at his watch,
pushing me to decide if the commanding general should just
review the parade by himself. We did go with the CG standing
out on the fifty-yard line solo. Dumb move.

I should've simply grabbed the city's "next in command."
Nobody got hurt or killed—but it would've been a nice gesture. I had just moved to the area and didn't even know who
all the players were—but that's no excuse if you're the PAO.

That inauspicious beginning of my relationship with the community fueled my desire to do much better in the future. When I left three years later, the Chamber of Commerce presented me with their "Member of the Year" plaque.

Train and brief your staff. Again, Cherry Point. I had received a call from the Air Station game warden not long before heading out for the aforementioned parade, alerting me that after weeks of trying alternative methods, he had shot, bagged, and disposed of several geese that were tearing up the golf course. ("Flying rodents," they're sometimes called, not to mention the bird strike danger they pose to jet aircraft.) At any rate, I failed to brief my number two, a young gunnery sergeant fairly new to public affairs, who got a call from the nearby ABC-TV affiliate. They asked about the geese, the gunny got the story from the game warden and then matter-of-factly told the television news director what he knew. No coordination. No context. No heads-up to the PAO or the command. We made Paul Harvey's nationally broadcast radio program with that one. Did I mention that the geese were the personal gift of a former Cherry Point commanding general?

The first I'd heard about us "going public" was when I saw the report on the 11 o'clock news, already having beaten myself up over my lack of situational awareness at Havelock High School earlier in the evening. We'd made some blunder or other in the Air Station newspaper, *The Windsock*, that day, as well. I told my sweet wife that her PAO husband had found a way a way to commit major local goofs from all three prongs of public affairs in one day.

Next morning I went in a little early, going straight to the command post. "Please tell the chief of staff I'm here with his breakfast," I told the staff secretary, pointing a cocked thumb at my chest. "Me!"

Col. Jack "Stinger" Hammond had seen and been through much worse, of course, and he simply laughed off the incident, knowing that the PAO was already working hard on clean-up ops.

Get organized! Many in the public affairs field are kinda artsy, creative, and passionate about their craft. They dream big dreams and have big visions. They're generally likable enough and certainly earnest, but when it comes to organization, dress-right-dress, and crossing t's and dotting i's—well, not so much. At least that's *my* story, and I may as well stick with it, since it's the truth.

I've been late for meetings, presented (or executed) ideas that were judged to be a little bit *too* far outside the box, and wasted way too much time retrieving important data because I failed to create and maintain an electronic (or other) system. Thank the Lord, none of my stupidity or disorganization ever got anybody killed.

My two favorite mess-ups, though, were attributable to my lack of double (or triple) checking dates and times. Major General Mize had laid on a very nice lunch at the Camp Lejeune Officers' Club with a very limited, exclusive cast of characters—the purpose being to explain his position, and secure buy-in, on an important land use issue.

Seated at the table were the general, the mayor, the local newspaper publisher, the president of the Chamber of Commerce—and the public affairs officer. Except I was nearly an hour late, having marked the wrong time in my "daytimer" or having neglected to even check it before slipping out for a nice noon jog. Ouch!

Gentleman that he is, General Mize never chided me for leaving our area's leading decision-makers waiting. His unspoken disappointment in me and my disappointment in myself created enough of a Robert E. Lee/Jeb Stuart moment to get the job done.

In 1990 I had Col. (later Brig. Gen.) Mike Hayes and the entire staff of Marine Forces Panama waiting for a postinvasion Professional Military Education (PME) lecture. We were to host the publisher and managing editor of the news-paper *El Siglo*. The Panama City tabloid had called for dictator Manuel Noriega's ouster long before it was cool—and they had paid the price, with broken arms and the publisher's home being blown up.

Good stuff for a PME on freedom of the press. Except I had the wrong day. After my third time checking the gate for our guests, I phoned them and confirmed from my own calendar that I had obviously blown it. They were very much looking forward to visiting with us the *following* day, as discussed. The colonel and my mates were understanding enough. We adjourned to the softball diamond or the officers' club (or both, as I recall) and recocked the ultimately very successful session the next day.

Best to under promise. In rural Jones County, North Carolina, a community activist was bent on getting some road improvements made in one of the poorer sections. He approached me about the possibility of the Cherry Point–based wing support squadron—with its bulldozers, graders, and other heavy equipment—conducting some "training" in the area to accomplish the task. Young Captain Oliver, after walking the ground with the gentleman and the squadron operations officer, allowed that this was certainly do-able and a pretty nice idea, at that. And I told him so. In writing. On command letterhead.

We eventually did that special community project—but not before the Jones County citizens were properly told "no" based on numerous, federal legal prohibitions. My poor CG at the time, Brig. Gen. Jake Vermilyea, was vilified by the local congressman and enjoyed quality face-time with the assistant commandant of the Marine Corps before we ironed it all out. I no longer doubt the veracity of official correspondence that explains that this or that error was caused by "a well-being but overzealous junior officer." I have *been* that junior officer.

Count the cost. The Joint Warfighting Center (JWFC) in Norfolk is a state-of-art operational exercise facility with all the bells and whistles you might hope for in training a three-star joint task force (JTF) to plan and execute its way through a major, international scenario. The JWFC provides everything but the people to man the spaces; that chore, including solicitation of assets from other services, is in the purview of the JTF commander's real world organization (in this case, the Second Marine Expeditionary Force, based in Camp Lejeune, North Carolina). The assumption is twenty-four-hour operations and, ultimately, each staff section is responsible for doing its own bean counting and recruiting.

Boy, did I underestimate!

Although we had fun with some outside-the-box foreign-language initiatives and took advantage of the opportunity to train up several subject matter experts from throughout the MEF, we were woefully undermanned.

A handful of hard-chargers scurried to do the work normally spread among a staff double in size. A couple of our key joint players were inexperienced, as well. These we put on the night shift (another bad decision), which meant that the frantic first hour of each morning was spent rewriting the slides and public affairs guidance that they'd done their best to construct.

During the very efficient hotwash at the end of the exercise, each staff lead gave one "thumbs up" and one "thumbs down" from his lessons-learned perspective. Remarking that "pain is the best teacher," I shared with the CG and the assembled masses that my good and bad points were wrapped up in the simple fact that I had failed to order up enough people. "The bad news," I reported, "is that during the course of the four-day exercise, everybody at some point had to play every position.

"But the good news is that everybody had the opportunity to play every position." (The good news for me is that I was in the service of yet another Robert E. Lee-type leader, Lt. Gen. Marty Berndt. Many only pay lip service to the risky notion of letting your people make, and learn from, their mistakes. But he was the real deal.)

Expect only what you inspect. New officers are taught the "Six Troop Leading Steps" at Quantico, with an emphasis on number six: "supervise." Neat idea. That does not mean you have to micromanage, but you have to ensure some form of quality control and follow-up as part of your system. So it was that I was getting a Saturday morning haircut at Darryl's Barbershop in Jacksonville, North Carolina. As Keisha clipped away, I was checking out my pride and joy, LCTV-10, the base television station that had a cable feed to the homes and businesses "out in town."

To my horror, I was watching a military morgue training film. And not just any military morgue. The graphic, detailed production, meant to demonstrate to Air Force and other morticians the way to handle a mass casualty situation, was filmed or taped in 1983. Our Camp Lejeune television station was showing some of the 241 dead Marines, sailors, and soldiers who had been killed in the terrorist attack of October 23, 1983, the tragic event sometimes called, simply, "The Beirut Bombing." The vast majority of the casualties, of course, came from Camp Lejeune, and that day had meanwhile come to define the special relationship that today exists between the base and Jacksonville and Onslow County. It would be hard for me to imagine a more insensitive piece of programming, given our location.

I called our television chief at home, who, after a seeming eternity of putzing with locks and keys and equipment, got the video off the screen and replaced it with the rotating "community calendar."

How did this happen in the first place? At my constant urging to secure free video products from the NFL, the History Channel, and various governmental and educational sources, my officer in charge came across some good sounding titles in an Air Force catalog. I forget what the title of the morgue training production was, but it did not bespeak the incredibly hurtful images that appeared on the TV screen in Darryl's Barbershop that day. And it certainly was never intended for general distribution or for entertainment. Thankfully, we never received any calls of complaint. People who live in and around North Carolina's "Crystal Coast" have better things to do on Saturday morning than watch TV.

Don't get ahead of yourself. "The identity of the service member is being withheld pending notification of next of kin." That familiar statement probably sums up the most sensitive aspect of military public affairs. This is a life and death business we're in, and we have to deal with those particular details more often than any of us would prefer.

The advent of Operation Iraqi Freedom, along with the official realization that many warriors' families (and extended families) are very geographically scattered, brought a new policy. Today, names are withheld an additional twenty-four hours *after* primary next of kin (NOK) have been properly notified that a loved one has died or been seriously injured. This is obviously not the kind of news that any family member—including grandparents, step-parents, or estranged relatives—wants to learn from CNN.

At any rate, we were operating under the old rules when Cherry Point housing was the scene of a murder-suicide in 1989. A military police SWAT team had surrounded the home in hopes of averting tragedy, but we learned later that the distraught Marine had actually done his killing hours earlier. Next day, the Marine Corps Exchange officer was kind enough to let me use his training room to host a news conference so that we would give area media a promised report on the tragic event.

As I prepared for the news conference, I knew that the Marine Corps lacked but one more notification. After I conferred with the casualty assistance officer, it seemed likely that the final official visit would be taking place momentarily, probably during the news conference.

So, I produced *two* versions of the news release I would be handing out at the press conference. Bad idea. Following our provost marshal's briefing to reporters and answering each and every question asked that morning, I checked one more time to see if NOK notification was complete. It was not, so I distributed what I thought was the news release without the victims' names, promising the assembled media that we would get back to them with that information as soon as it was releasable.

"Keith, did you know there's a name on this release?" asked *Havelock News* editor Fran Hume.

Red-faced, I quickly collected the news releases and gave the media the version I should have given them in the first place. They were all understanding and I thanked them for that—especially Fran. To those PAOs who have told me that the media can never be your friends, I would humbly suggest: let me know how that works out for you.

When you're not the sharpest knife in the drawer, as is my challenge, you need all the help you can get. Meantime, I don't do double news releases any more. Even when contingencies require a rough "Plan B" or even a "Plan C," I guard those "what if" working papers with my life.

Call first. The chief of staff at Parris Island was kind enough when he phoned to school me on professional courtesy that afternoon. First Lieutenant Oliver had just escorted a television crew to the commissary to tape some innocuous story. The chief and the commissary manager both acknowledged that the media's request was legitimate and their televised product would likely do no harm—but a little coordination would've been nice. It was the last time I "just showed up" with the media, or any guest, without giving my hosts a heads-up.

Gremlins at the printing plant. Proofreading, or lack of same, happens to everybody, especially in print journalism. Actually, broadcast journalism, too, as evidenced by Defense Information School colleague, Dr. Dave Phillips, and his unfortunate, on-air mispronunciation of former NFL great Tucker Frederickson's name, back in Dave's sportscasting days.

But I digress.

The editor of the world-famous Camp Lejeune *Globe* was no doubt trying to lend a little class to our weekly base newspaper. The photograph depicted the commanding general of the Second Force Service Support Group pouring coffee—from a silver service, no less—for some senior officers visiting from Denmark.

The caption read, "Tea and Strumpets." Our horrified editor, Sgt. Victoria Gross, had meant, of course, for the copy to read, "crumpets."

I've known devilishly good-humored Maj. Gen. Bob Dickerson for many years, so I informed him of the goof with a different tack than I may have chosen for some other commanders. "General," I told him over the phone, just after the newspaper had hit the streets, "we've got a problem with the Norgies."

"How's that, Keith?" he asked.

"Well, sir," I told him. "If you'll turn to page 17 in your *Globe* this morning, you'll see a photo of you offering 'tea and strumpets' to those visiting Danes.

"This has upset the Norwegian delegation; they're claiming all you gave them were some pastries and a commemorative coin."

I truthfully told my hard-charging staff that morning and, on a few other occasions, that they had yet to make a mistake I had not made myself—usually with more grandeur and much more publicly.

Being there. It was late at night when the call came and I was just in from a trip. A helicopter had crashed in the waters on the south side of base near Sneads Ferry, and there were casualties. One of my captains was on duty and was already on scene. It was a tough day or so for all concerned, and public affairs wise, the media handled the story with great decorum and sensitivity.

But the morning after the crash, my commanding general phoned to ask why I had not been at the scene. He and I had been in the woods together the night an Osprey went down a few weeks before, and I had been able to give my boss some logistics support and on-site public affairs counsel before he faced the television cameras.

I told the general, regarding the more current crisis, that I had faith in my skipper and that I wanted to stay out of his hair. I allowed, though, that I still could've been present to lend moral support.

I should've been there.

The balance piece. The good news in the PAO biz is that you're never done. That is, you often have the opportunity for a "redo," a clarification, a correction, an edited version. At the very least, the chance to get it right the next time.

But the bad news is, also, that you're never done.

For the sake of your family, those whom you lead and for your own physical, mental, and emotional well-being, you must have a life outside of this particular kind of work. And, you've got to demonstrate the discipline to "turn it off" sometimes.

Believe it or not, the much-ballyhooed "twenty-four-hour news cycle" can get along without you for a few days. And when (not if) things go wrong, and something stinky and ugly is plastered all over the front page, you may be the guy whose job is to remind everybody of the temporal nature of the problem. Folks'll be wrapping fish in that newspaper the very next day.

There's a time when you want to strive for perfection for a particular event, a news conference, a special project. But there is also a time when "the 80 percent solution" answers the mail. As a leader involved in public affairs, it's up to you to figure out which is which. That's why you get paid the big bucks.

Extra hint: Your wife's birthday and your anniversary get more than the 80 percent solution. (For some more practical tips on maintaining that balance, check out "A Dichotomy Oversold" in the appendix).

Don't get slick with the media. My first month at Camp Lejeune we dealt with the relief and court-martial of a captain in the Marine Combat Training Battalion. I don't recall all the circumstances, but I remember we chose to "hit send" on the faxed news release right at quitting time on a Friday, a tactic normally relegated to goings-on in Washington, D.C., and executed for the purpose of low-keying whatever news or announcement you're not particularly proud of. I was cured of that spinmeister tactic when our news release went out with an error, promptly posted by the Associated Press. Capt. Shawn Turner and I then spent much of Friday night trying to fix our miscue, working with AP's skeleton weekend crew and learning more about their correction process than we cared to know.

Much better is the straight-up approach I saw modeled by Lt. Gen. Rusty Blackman when he commanded the Second Marine Division. One of his senior U.S. Navy medical officers had been relieved for conduct unbecoming an officer and several, more serious charges involving patient abuse. General Blackman rejected out of hand the notion of punting the affair over to the Navy. "That would be disingenuous," he said. "The Doc is one of ours. We'll deal with it."

Don't let 'em egg you on. The *Savannah Morning News* reporter was insistent when he called me about 2 AM, and this was probably our fifth or sixth telephone conversation in the last twenty-four hours. A Marine gunnery sergeant had been apprehended by military police for allegedly murdering his infant son, in his crib, at the gunny's Parris Island government quarters.

The military justice system, like any justice system, must follow certain procedures; and this journalist was not being a cooperative student as I tried to painstakingly explain those procedures.

"Whaddya mean he hasn't been officially charged yet?" the reporter asked, incredulously. "Does that mean you people have got him running loose?"

"Look," I told him, through clenched teeth, "Turner's in the brig and he's not going anywhere."

The pull-quote, positioned on the front page, above the fold, was attributed to "Base Spokesman" and, of course, read: "Turner's in the brig and he's not going anywhere."

While "open and shut" cases are not necessarily the norm, this time it was. The only question mark was in sentencing a few weeks later (the Marine ultimately received the death penalty, later commuted to life in prison by the Marine Corps Recruit Depot commander, Maj. Gen. Stephen Olmstead).

Had there been any legal doubts, however, my rash and careless statement as official spokesman would've given the defense attorney legitimate reason to cry "command influence." My error in judgment was kindly chalked up to youthful inexperience by the CG and my boss, Maj. Jim Vance.

For Your Rucksack

Besides the grace of God and the patient, often good-humored understanding of some wonderful senior leaders, what saved me in spite of inevitable fumbles and interceptions was, I hope, a career-long emphasis on being a team player—being a Marine, first.

If your boss knows clearly that you are "in the fight," that you cheerfully pull your load within the command and look for ways to improve and contribute, there is much room for forgiveness (despite the bumper stickers and office plaques about "Marine Corps policy" that state otherwise).

As with bad news that you must report to the media: own up to it, as quickly as possible—and communicate the positive steps you are taking to avoid repeating the offense.

Appendix 1

AGGRESSIVENESS 101

Our concepts and organizations must be redesigned
to use technology effectively, informed by historical
experience . . .

— GENERAL JAMES L. JONES

Back to the Future in Public Affairs

By Col. Keith Oliver*

If Our Corps Is to Capitalize on Recent Public
Affairs Accomplishments, Then Robust Application
of Some of Our Classic Favorites—Including Radio
and Renewed Hometown Emphasis—Is in Order

—COL. KEITH OLIVER

As Americans have come to expect, Marine Corps contributions to Operations Enduring Freedom and Noble Eagle have not gone unnoticed. Images of disciplined, desert-cammied Marines ranging over the Afghan countryside were a television news staple when the Leathernecks first rode into this Global War on Terrorism. Back home, appreciative audiences heard commanders articulate what the newly formed 4th Marine Expeditionary Brigade (Anti-Terrorism) was doing in Little Rock, Arkansas. And if Devil Dogs weren't presenting the "Top Ten List" on *Late Night with David Letterman*, they were getting married on Regis Philbin's show or singing "God Bless America" for the opening of the New York Stock Exchange.

Behind the scenes, especially in the field environment, imaginative, mostly company grade, Marine PAOs and NCOs got the message out by hook or by crook, using a blend of technology and chutzpah.

Well before 9/11, satellites, cell phones, e-mail, and the internet had been playing an increasingly important role in Marine Corps Public Affairs. So great has been the technological explosion that a webmaster MOS should probably *already* be part of the training pipeline. And television, coming soon to a base near you as part of a developing Marine Corps network, has probably received more funding in the last year than it did in the previous ten.

But we can't fall in love with the technology. Rather, as has always been the case with our grunt brethren, it's that Marine trademark aggressive spirit—that "fire in the belly"—that needs to drive our public affairs programs.

Passing the Torch

Marine Sgt. Neil Gillespie, a World War II combat photographer, exhibited these traits when famed U.S. aviation pioneer Capt. Eddie Rickenbacker and six companions were lost in the South Pacific, surviving in an open raft for twenty-four days. The enterprising NCO snapped the first photos of Rickenbacker when he was rescued, nabbing a big spread in *Life* magazine. Short on photographic equipment, Gillespie improvised: he rigged a flash from the refractor of a Seabee bulldozer headlight and, Pony Express style, placed the film canister in the hands of a Navy pilot for delivery to Samoa.

Sgt. Gillespie's approach to his duties (he sometimes souped his film in a discarded Corsair fuel tank) is reflected in the institution's current Marine Corps Public Affairs mission statement, with its overt emphasis on proactiveness and creativity. BGen Robert L. Denig Sr. and "Denig's Demons," the Corps' first combat correspondents and PAOs, would be pleased.

The original CCs' pathway to success was, first and always, through a Marine's hometown, that mainstay of American journalism that always asks for the local angle; that always begs the question, "what does this event mean to me?" The venerable *Associated Press Styleguide* devotes an entire section to the hometown, and editorial instructions require that a reporter always obtain the subject's full name, age, and hometown. It's even a source of civic pride when, owing to population and certain other criteria, a city rates listing in the *Styleguide sans* state, e.g., Chicago, Tampa, Baltimore.

Radio, TV, and even the web are no less localized; they're just under exploited.

Bottom line: the Marine Corps as a *Citizen Kanesque* media mogul just doesn't fit. Sure, we'll get the *Time* cover and the *Washington Post* front page, but our bread and butter has been, and must remain, that same "single, well-aimed round" that characterizes Marine marksmanship. Leap-ahead technology, in public affairs or any other enterprise, is rendered ineffective if we trip over the obvious—something we must not do with radio (read: "drive time!"). How many among our internal and external audiences, after all, are watching television, surfing the web, or reading the newspaper in their automobiles?

Going much further back in Marine Corps history, the Green Machine's intrinsic ties to the Navy are showing new signs of life among the operators (unprecedented engagement and cooperation *vis-à-vis* amphibious ready groups, tactical aircraft, littoral warfare, etc.). In the public affairs domain, the Navy-Marine Team funded a successful print and film awareness advertising campaign and debuted a 1940s-style, 4 and 1/2 minute "newsreel" in 2,000 motion-picture theaters nationwide this fall.

Let's not stop there. With the rebirth of Air-Naval Gunfire Liaison (ANGLICO) teams, a public affairs/combat camera version could be an Amphibious Ready Group asset, combining Navy-Marine tools and manpower to bring America even more robust coverage of her warriors' activities out there on freedom's edge. Back home, we can help cement blue-green relations with a very simple set of exchange tours: a Navy photojournalist or broadcaster would join the rosters of our largest public affairs shops, i.e., Camp Pendleton, Camp Lejeune, and Okinawa, each of which enjoy a sizable U.S. Navy population. The exchange? Marine combat correspondent NCOs at the Naval Academy and Pensacola, two venues steeped in proud and unique Marine Corps traditions but which have been virtually silent from a Corps public affairs perspective.

A View from Today's PAO Fighting Hole

Defense Department and Marine Corps public affairs policy covers a lot of ground, but from a practical standpoint, and especially during wartime, the body of doctrine and public affairs guidance (the ubiquitous PAG) offers two simple notions: (1) to get civilian news media to the fight and (2) to ensure their product gets out.

If that's so, why send Marines to college-level schooling to learn print and broadcast journalism? Three reasons:

1. Informed, educated media escorts are more effective media escorts; they understand deadlines, sound checks, and camera angles.

2. You never know. On occasion, usually because of proximity or security clearance or possession of a current backseat card, the military journalist is the only trained news professional on-scene at a particular tactical event, often one of momentous importance. More than one Marine has garnered a magazine cover shot by being at the right place at the right time (and at Tarawa, Sgt. Norm Hatch's documentary footage won the young Leatherneck an Academy Award in 1944!).

3. We feed media product to the "great middle"—those newspapers and broadcast outlets that are neither located right outside the base's main gate, nor have the reach and budget of, say, *The New York Times*. But they will hungrily devour the words and pictures that Marine combat correspondents can provide, particularly when a robust hometown angle is part of the service.

We outsmart ourselves when we don't pay attention to that "great middle." (That's "low-hanging fruit," as former Director of Public Affairs, Maj. Gen. Cliff Stanley, is fond of saying). Anytime we become too sophisticated to devote due attention to weekly newspapers, smalltown dailies, and AM (as well as FM) radio, we're "giving up the short game."

Another disingenuous pothole is to suppose that public affairs activity is relegated to the arena of policy and planning. It is not. For both officer and enlisted, this is blue-collar work to be done with ink-stained hands; and if the Annex F does not result in headlines, news bites, and, yes, hometown clippings, somebody is not doing his job.

Worse is the highbrow insistence by some that the PAO exists only to *inform*; that he should never engage in tawdry offshoots that reek of "influencing," "marketing," "publicity," or "selling. " Baloney. If the public affairs officer is not aggressively promoting his command, his community, and his Corps from the time he gets up in the morning, then somebody needs to check his pulse.

Taking Care of Our Livestock

Owing in part to its small population (128 active duty officers; 363 enlisted), career management in public affairs has been painful, at best. The institution unceremoniously did away with warrant officers in the early 1990s, it routinely fills colonel billets with majors, and, for years, burned out promising PAOs by simply moving them from one public affairs job to the next, with little hope for the personal and professional growth that comes with career broadening tours. Even school assignments were looked at with a jaundiced eye by some harried, misguided occfield sponsors who had the unenviable task of "filling holes."

"We beat up our young PAOs," Deputy Commandant for Plans, Policies, and Operations, Lt. Gen. "Buck" Bedard has said. "And they get discouraged."

The situation has improved somewhat with Maj.Gen. Stanley and Maj. "Doc" Church's drive to begin "mainstreaming the MOS" in 1996. Today, company-grade PAOs can compete for the opportunity to instruct at The Basic School in addition to a wider array of "B" billets that run the gamut from possible Naval Academy or NROTC assignment to graduate education, to command—perhaps at a recruit depot. Another important new wrinkle keeps two captains on staff at college-accredited Defense Information School. There, the skippers not only have the opportunity to mold young minds in the classroom; they are assured of a twelve-month command stint (as MarDet CO).

Moreover, they can point to a 4302 major who presently serves as a recruiting station CO and another major who is participating in a specially tailored year-out program with Tribune Company (Los Angeles' KTLA-TV, *Chicago Tribune*, *Newsday*, et al.). Further up the line, a selected colonel was recently assigned to the Vice-Chairman's staff, one of the most senior public affairs jobs to be held by a career Marine PAO. Hopeful signs, all.

On the enlisted side, motivated combat correspondents have done successful, career-enhancing turns as drill instructors or recruiters for many years, in addition to Marine Security Guard and other duties. And a Staff NCO year-out program hits the streets next year, placing a seasoned enlisted warrior on the staff of a major marketing firm. The Corps does, however, owe some of these hard-chargers the opportunity to serve as warrant officers; and the institution needs their expertise.

Choice "B" billets aside, the onus remains on the individual Marine, officer or enlisted, to seek and exploit less obvious opportunities for growth. A handout once passed out by the Marine Corps Representative at Defense Information School, speaks to a mind-set that would well serve a young Marine leader in any of the Corps' low-population, non-combat arms, military occupational specialties ("the boutique MOSs," Brig. Gen. Mike Lehnert calls them). Particularly for officers, the cultivation of a broad view of the battlefield is just as desirable today as it was when wooden ships sailed the seas.

There are no magic bullets in this article—and it's probably unlawful to issue any on behalf of an MOS that sardonically clings to its World War II motto, "Last to Know, First to Go." Instead, this is an exhortation for public affairs practitioners—and those who command them—to unabashedly celebrate the colorful, make-it-happen heritage that earmarks the Marine fighter.

"Although painful to acknowledge," wrote Col. John Greenwood in a thoughtful editorial in the March 1988 *Marine Corps Gazette*, "taking innovative action aggressively and on one's own responsibility is not a universal Marine characteristic."

But it needs to be.

More than new programs, more than funding, more than gear, more than battalions of fresh combat correspondents, Marine Corps Public Affairs needs but to look back. The tribal elders of this warrior-scribe MOS set an adventurous course marked by improvisation, guts, and tenacity. And their lock on the hometown presses of America demonstrated a clear, active understanding of the campaign adage voiced by the late House Speaker Tip O'Neill: "All politics are local."

---

*Reprinted from the March 2003 *Marine Corps Gazette*, with permission.

Appendix 2

A GENERAL SAYS TO "OPEN IT UP" WITH THE MEDIA

Stop Whining

By Gen. Walt Boomer*

When I was asked to appear on this panel, I asked myself: Why are we doing this again? How many panels have we had on the military and the media? I bring a little different view to this whole subject, and that is, if we haven't figured this out yet on the military side and on the media side, we're not half as smart as I think we are.

From the military perspective, there is something we need to understand. This is a democracy. And a free press is the fundamental underpinning of everything that we stand for, fight for, and believe in. Now, it doesn't make any difference then whether you like the media or you don't like the media—they're here to stay.

It's the same situation that I face now as the leader of a public company. I may or may not like the Wall Street analysts who cover our company, and may or may not like the view that they take, which is sometimes short-term versus long-term, but, too bad. I can't change that. I have to deal with analysts because they are there and it's my responsibility to figure out how to deal with them.

It's the military's responsibility to figure out how to deal with the media, and the Admiral (Rear Admiral Brent Baker, USN, retired) just suggested some ways. I think it is a healthy thing for the American military to be exposed through the media to the public. After all, they pay our salaries. Now, there are legitimate securities issues, but they're another question, and we all understand it.

So, to the military I would say: Look, figure out a way to deal with this problem. Stop talking about it, stop whining about it, just get down to work. I tell my people now that talk is cheap, plans are cheap. If it doesn't translate into work, I don't want to hear about it.

Let's stop talking about this issue and solve it. It's not that big a deal. From the media side, you are, you always will be a pain in the neck. It has been that way and it is going to be that way in the future. You are a burden when you come out to call on us. That doesn't mean that we should exclude you, but you are a burden. You take up time in a person's very, very busy day.

If I know that I'm a burden, I try to act a little bit differently and appreciate the fact that I am a burden. But in wartime, you should be able to cover the war. The American people need to know what's happening and what's going on. In this information age, they need to see and to understand, as horrible as it might be, what is happening on the battlefield. Perhaps, if more people understood the horror, we would be less inclined to go to war. And my message to the media is the same as it is to the military: Stop whining about it. We can't take all of the media at the same time. The thousands that might descend upon the battlefield can't be dealt with. So let's figure out way to deal with what we can deal with, and then let's have the courage to talk about the security issue. There are some things that cannot be broadcast, should not be broadcast, because there are legitimate security reasons for not doing so. We just need to figure out what they are—and they're not very hard

On the military side, however, don't use security as a cop out. There are relatively few things that the press cannot be told, relatively few things.

Now, that's how I feel about it. And because I felt that way about it, that is why we operated the way we did during Desert Shield and Desert Storm. The First Marine Expeditionary Force was open to the media. We had laid out some rules—I didn't like them all—but they caused us to be able to deal with fewer rather than more media. But those [reporters] that got out, we welcomed them. They could go anywhere, do anything, talk to anybody, from private to general, no restraints, no restrictions.

Now, there's a caveat here, if you're going to do that, you better have faith in your troops. If you don't trust them, if you don't have faith in them, you can't turn the media loose. But I would submit that if you don't have faith in them and don't trust them, you're not a very good leader and you shouldn't be there either. You've got to be able to deal with the one percent that is going to say what you don't want them to say. There's going to be one Marine, one Sailor who is going to embarrass you, but only one. Ride that storm out; don't shut it down because of the one percent.

There's been a lot of discussion of Molly Moore's [*Washington Post* reporter] coverage of the war. In fact, I noticed the picture of Molly Moore and me in front of my tent when we came back from the attack in Kuwait [in the May 1997 *Proceedings*]. You should know that I extended that invitation to five reporters. Molly was the only one who showed up. This wasn't the fault of the other people; it was rather late in the campaign planning when I decided to do this, and then there were some who thought, "Boomer's going to be fifty miles behind the lines and there ain't going to be any story there." Well, they didn't know me very well, but that's how Molly happened to get the scoop.

Both sides need to stop talking about this thing, sit down, and get to work, figure out the few tough issues that we need to work on and let's learn to live together. Neither of us is going to go away.

---

*From the July 1997 *Proceedings*. Reprinted with permission.

Appendix 3

PLENTY BUSY BACK HOME

Meanwhile, Back at the Ranch

By Maj. Keith Oliver*

P ublic affairs during Operation Desert Storm was as fla-
vorful and challenging as in other recent real-time envi-
ronments and has already generated lively debate on
issues ranging from civilian media access to internal audiovisual support. But one important aspect—public relations/
support on the homefront—should not be excluded from the
Corps' retrospectives.

On the local, base-community relations level, especially, this
undertaking, the biggest since World War II, called for a public
affairs effort that was sensitive, aggressive, and creative. Above
all, it needed the hands-on involvement of senior commanders. As a case in point, "back at the ranch" in Havelock, North
Carolina, home to Marine Corps Air Station Cherry Point and
the 2d Marine Aircraft Wing (MAW), it would appear that the
mail was answered.

Havelock and the surrounding area defies the "military
town" stereotype; a base information guide labels the relationship between the air station and base as "unique in all
the Corps." The closeness, family atmosphere, and retired
Marine influence played in the respective commanding generals' decision to be especially aggressive and enthusiastic
in keeping the populace informed about Desert Shield and
Desert Storm developments.

Two full-blown news conferences, one in August and a
second in January, offered as much detail as prudently possible about Cherry Point's activity as a major aerial port of

embarkation and the commanding general, 2d MAWs, role as the Marine Corps worldwide air movement control officer, in addition to sending his own substantial numbers of people and aircraft. (It should be noted here that Cherry Point is the headquarters location for Marine Corps Air Bases Eastern Area as well as for the 2d MAW. Both major commands have subordinate units at New River, North Carolina, and Beaufort, South Carolina, thus efforts chronicled here are representative of activity at three Marine Corps Air Stations.)

In many ways, the corresponding meetings with area civilian officials held here were more significant than the two major news conferences. The same ground was covered, but in advance—a point not lost on the appreciative mayors, city managers, and other community leaders. Both of Cherry Point's resident commanding generals, Maj. Gen. Richard D. Hearney and Brig. Gen. David A. Richwine, briefed the committee-sized group, offering maps, charts, and slides along with a comprehensive question-and-answer session.

The generals also sent their community plans and liaison officer, Col. David Nelson, "on the road," hitting seemingly every Rotary Club between I-95 and the Atlantic Coast. If the area was threatened (and, indeed, it was struck) by some pretty serious economic woes, at least there was no information drought. The Marines, by far the region's largest employer, accurately came across as friendly and upfront neighbors, sharing every precious bit of news available. Other initiatives in the three-pronged public affairs attack are outlined below:

Internal Information

- Recognizing that civilian media outlets were often more effective (certainly more timely) vehicles for reaching internal audiences, i.e., Marine families, than was the command newspaper. "Internal" was also assumed to mean internal to the Marine Corps, hence a strong push to feed other base newspapers and Defense-oriented publications with timely information.

- Obtaining "family grams" and other informal communication from deploying commands for the purpose of wider, follow-on circulation through news releases and publication in the station newspaper.

- Holding one-on-one sessions with deploying unit information officers (collateral duty public affairs officers) and discussing ways in which we could help them publicize the activities of their squadron, thus keeping family and friends updated. A cargo pocketful of black-and-white and color film was always provided to help the process get started.

- Gleaning highlights from wire service stories (basic avoid-plagiarism rules applied) and establishing a local tie-in to world events whenever possible. This was particularly important in the absence of timely products "from the field" during the early going. Later, civilian media "pool products" from in-theater were used and fully justified, given the fact that it was Marine sweat and muscle that made their distribution possible in the first place. A special challenge hampering internal efforts was the Pentagon's insistence that all audiovisual products, including still photographs shot at home bases, had to go to the large black hole in Washington before they could be published or televised. The result: even innocuous, unclassified—but heartwarming—pictures shot by military video technicians had difficulty seeing the light of day. Some common sense next time, please.

- Realizing that part of "internal information" is preparing Marines and their families to deal with "external information." Classes and printed crib sheets that pointed out some of the rocks and shoals in dealing with the civilian press were made available.

External Information

- Providing fact sheets, unit histories, and commanding officers' photos and biographies to hungry media. File footage of deploying aircraft and generic Middle East maps were provided, as well.

- Offering a "media opportunity of the day" during the intense week-long periods in August and December. Alternating among various squadrons and the wing's two battalions, journalists were able to record a wide variety of colorful activity with minimal operational interference. Each visit received a front-page, top-of-the-news splash, and a Marine duty expert was always available for on-camera, on-the-record comments.

- Emphasizing the Desert Shield/Storm was not the Corps' be-all and end-all. We had a nice turnout, for example, for the earlier-than-planned sendoff of an Intruder squadron to the Far East, stressing the Corps' constants of readiness and global commitment.

- Arranging for local press to visit the theater of operations under the Defense Department's "hometown media program," which gave credit where it was due. This was a welcome Washington-generated idea whose time had come. Months later, those fortunate enough to have made the trip were still smiling in the after-glow-Marines-at-heart, each one.

Community Relations

- Acknowledging area citizens' many and varied shows of support. These included displaying enough yellow ribbon to gift-wrap an LHA and throwing a military family day in the park that still has people talking. Commanders saluted their civilian neighbors via luncheon speeches, letters-to-the-editor, and through personal, one-on-one communication.

- Arranging to get a North Carolina flag to the troops and publicizing its presentation (by State Sen. Beverly Perdue) and display in Saudi Arabia by tarheel natives assigned to deployed 2d MAW units.
- Presenting framed photographs to city hall and the Chamber of Commerce that showed the official Havelock license plate being affixed to a desert-cammied HMMWV by a homegrown Marine in the Middle East
- Making Marines available to visit schools, churches, and civic organizations to offer insight as to the local warriors' mission "over there."

Mostly, it seemed, the Navy-Marine Team in eastern North Carolina was in a receive mode in terms of community relations. Local hospitals, schools, churches, and businesses were forever calling their armed brethren to offer specific support, such as free telephones for key wife programs, specific ministries to assist families of deployed Marines, or the hiring of special school counselors to help military juniors deal with the dangers of war. All this came from folks who were sustaining obvious economic hurt in a town that sent far more than half its economic base off to the sound of guns.

And they were thanked in person by President Bush himself. I landed in Saudi the day he addressed Cherry Point and Havelock from a banner-festooned hangar. I got to hear him praise that faithful and very special North Carolina community on Armed Forces Radio while rolling down the road in a desert caravan. It was with the deepest sense of justice and satisfaction that I heard those who had given so much being recognized by their national leader.

President Bush particularly noted what area residents now know as "the flame," a quickly planned and executed symbol at City Park, erected just after the Baghdad bombing started, meant to show that Havelock "keeps the home fires burning."

At this writing, well after the season of spirited homecomings and citizen-generated celebrations, Havelock and Cherry Point have returned to relative normalcy, but the well-greased communication lines between Marines and civilians continue to get a good workout. Public affairs planning, sometimes off-the-cuff but always in written form with staff input, set a framework for capitalizing on this period of good will toward the fighting man.

Often, the details made the difference: making sure to get extra copies of regional newspapers for mailing to the troops overseas; demonstrating civilian support by soliciting and publicizing VIP quotes; giving at least equal treatment to hometown media, even when media "big boys" from Washington and elsewhere came to call.

Finally, I need to make an important note about manpower. The influx of media, coupled with Fleet Marine Force commitments that sent a good chunk of local Marines either to the sand or elsewhere, created a challenge. During peak periods, this obstacle was overcome with Marine Reserves' help, a volunteer dependent wife who joined the Windsock staff, and especially a pair of local retired public affairs staff noncommissioned officers who unselfishly offered up their combined fifty years' experience in escorting media, handling calls, and generally holding down the fort.

---

*Reprinted from the October 1992 *Marine Corps Gazette*, with permission.

Appendix 4

EMBEDDED MEDIA CAN'T DO IT ALL

Journalists in Uniform

By Keith Oliver*

In war and peace, the mainstay of a commander's public affairs program is a trained and influential force of enlisted journalists and photographers.

The battle-tested practice of embedding media is all the rage these days in the war reporter biz. Never mind that the concept predates Ernie Pyle, or that its execution during Operation Iraqi Freedom was less than perfect. A win is a win—and the American public benefited from a troops' eye view of Operation Iraqi Freedom in the spring of 2002.

But as with any operational success, those with their finger on the pulse must take care not to draw the wrong lessons from the program's rave reviews. Specifically, joint combat leaders at every level must be certain not to cavalierly or unknowingly jettison a critical piece of the public affairs arsenal already in place: the enlisted combat correspondent (CC).

Make no mistake: Defense Department policy is correctly weighted toward getting civilian news media to the fight and, when necessary, assisting them in getting their stories and pictures out. Since at least 1941, however, a population of enlisted journalists, photographers, and broadcasters has been resourced, trained, and deployed to tell their services' (and America's) story day in and day out. These men and women are the offensive line: steady producers who often cede the spotlight to the "Gunga Dan" Rathers of the world when the balloon goes up.

A cursory look at current official military websites shows a robust emphasis on solid media products done by our uniformed combat correspondents—a marked improvement over output during the "major combat" phase in Iraq where this precious resource was vastly underutilized. One PAO, it was reported, expressly forbade one of his NCOs from writing and shooting photographs, telling the enlisted man that "(your) only job is to escort news media."

Every fight from WWII forward has seen the work of enlisted CCs occasionally picked up by the wire services, including front-page photography in national publications—a simple case of being in the right place at the right time. But their bread and butter is "flyover country," where Middle America particularly depends on military journalists and photographers to send news back home. These citizens' smaller-market print and broadcast outlets simply don't have the manpower and budget resources to sign up at the embed table.

The CCs' civilian counterparts seem to appreciate their battlefield colleagues' unique position. As *Dallas Morning News* writer David Flick said of Cpl. Joel Chaverri, whose unit fought in Fallujah, "(his) assignment . . . requires him to write accurately and photograph well—and to return fire whenever fired upon."

"Some reporters try to distance themselves from what they cover," wrote Flick of his fellow Texan. "Joel Chaverri doesn't have that option." Nor should savvy employment of our combat correspondents be optional in any conflict or contingency.

Defense Information School (DINFOS) equips the young specialists well to be able to work alongside and assist their civilian counterparts. Initial training, followed by assignments aboard our ships, posts, and stations, render hands-on appreciation for deadlines, photo angles, and other aspects of print and broadcast journalism.

Such value to civilian journalists who find themselves covering American forces is really a by-product, since military men and women assigned to what academia calls the "communications arts" are storytellers in their own right. They received college credit for their coursework at DINFOS and their newscasts, photographs, bylines, and artwork reach a wide audience on a weekly and, often, daily basis.

Besides, it doesn't take special school training to escort news media (especially those already folded-in with a unit) any more than it does to escort politicians, contractors, or humanitarian aid workers.

Not that there are enough public affairs types to go around in the first place, which is why the very best of them strive to be fully engaged in all facets of their craft, especially when forward-deployed. The editor of *Homeland Defense Journal,* retired Marine Maj. Robert T. Jordan, is a case in point.

Best known as the PAO on the ground when the Marine Barracks blew on that infamous Sunday morning of October 23, 1983, Jordan had been a staff sergeant in Vietnam. "I was initially assigned as a press escort from early July 1968 through March 1969," he said, "(but) it was humbling to find that I was selected for this duty not because of any superior communications skills but because of my previous experience as a Marine infantryman and hand-to-hand combat instructor.

"I resented the assignment until Col. Paul Moriarity bought me dinner at the CIB (Command Information Bureau) one evening and explained the importance of what I was doing, shared the many compliments that he had received on my assistance to the news crews, and reminded me that I was not restricted from reporting on my own.

"Thereafter," Jordan said, "I carried a sketch pad, tape recorder, note pad, and camera on every escort mission. Once I finished assisting the (civilian) correspondents in getting the stories they wanted, I sketched, photographed, interviewed, and wrote to my heart's content."

In Afghanistan last spring where combat operations were largely overshadowed by events in Iraq, Gunnery Sgt. Keith Milks adapted the same entrepreneurial mindset to the opposite situation. "Freed from the task of constantly arranging logistics for and escorting civilian media," he wrote in the November 2004 *Marine Corps Gazette,* "the MEU's public affairs section was able to devote most of its time to telling firsthand the story of the unit's role in Operation Enduring Freedom—a story that might not otherwise have been told."

The story was told, all right, via the 22d MEU's website and through some seven hundred news products released direct to print and broadcast outlets at home and abroad. (And the hands-on gunny practiced what he preached; not only did he write prolifically, his combat photos landed on the covers of a half-dozen magazines.)

Soon enough, civilian news media "clamored to join our ranks," said Milks, especially after MEU combat correspondents had faithfully documented their unit's success in killing eighty Taliban and other enemy in one week. A short time later when Operation Thunder Road commenced, the six-man public affairs team was "deluged with requests from reporters."

The same talent pool that gives us hard chargers like Jordan and Milks is also responsible for the ubiquitous base newspaper and other "command information" or "internal information" tools. The media content is largely the same as that bound for an ostensibly "external" audience, another area where the worldwide web and other means have dramatically increased the overlap among and between traditional public affairs functions.

In any case, the skills are in evidence and crisp writing and photography are annually recognized by the Defense Department's Thomas Jefferson Awards Program, the U.S. Marine Corps Combat Correspondents Association and others. Many in the pen-and-sword club have obtained a certain notoriety, particularly overseas or at remote stateside locations, perhaps anchoring the news for the Far East Network or writing sports in the football-crazy South.

Former Air Force NCO Adrian Cronauer, portrayed by Robin Williams in *Good Morning, Vietnam*, comes to mind, as does onetime soldier-writer Neil Sheehan (*A Bright Shining Lie*), Coast Guard journalist, the late Alex Haley (*Roots*), or former Marine Chas Henry, national security correspondent for Washington's WTOP radio. Even game show meister Pat Sajak got his start in uniform, as an Army broadcast specialist in Vietnam.

Each of these former news junkie grunts is an example of influence wielded in their civilian careers—but they also cut a wide swath as relatively junior service members. As a demographic, the very manageable number of military print and broadcast journalists should represent a key target audience for organizations like the U.S. Naval Institute, that aspires to gain new members and greater visibility throughout the forces.

Is every warrior-scribe or photographer Pulitzer Prize-Winning material? No. Neither is every embedded reporter. But a goodly number of our youngsters in Iraq and elsewhere are crackerjack writers and shooters. To be condescending or patronizing to those who ride the military "press bus" is folly. The smartest commands and affiliate organizations look beyond the traditional flag officer and trade media invitation list to ensure that these special petty officers and corporals (and the chiefs and gunnies who guide them) are read-in on new programs and policy initiatives.

Reach your enlisted public affairs force and you "reach the fleet." Scratch that. Reach them and you reach the *world*.

---

*Published in the August 2005 Naval Institute *Proceedings*. Reprinted with permission.

Appendix 5

LOTS TO DO—WITH OR WITHOUT THE SPOTLIGHT

22d MEU Public Affairs in the Forgotten War
MEV PAO Sections Are Responsible for Getting the Word Out

By GySgT. Keith A. Milks*

When the 22d Marine Expeditionary Unit (Special Operations Capable) (22d MEU-SOC) pushed deep into Afghanistan's Oruzgan Province in the spring of 2004, the attention of the world media was focused elsewhere. An alleged prisoner abuse scandal in Iraq, high-profile rape and murder cases, surging gas prices, and a tumultuous U.S. presidential campaign dominated news headlines.

The ongoing campaign in Afghanistan, where the first shots in the war against terror were fired in late 2001, had all but dropped off the radar as Operation Iraqi Freedom replaced Enduring Freedom at the forefront of American consciousness. In fact, the feature story in the March 8 edition of *Time* magazine was appropriately titled, "Remember Afghanistan?"

Although Cable News Network, Fox News, and several other national and international news agencies did report on some of the 22d MEU's combat and civil military operations, the lack of intense civilian media coverage presented the MEU's correspondents and combat cameramen a unique opportunity.

Freed from the task of constantly arranging logistics for and escorting civilian media, the MEU's public affairs (PA) section was able to devote most of its time to telling firsthand the story of the unit's role in Operation Enduring Freedom—a story that might not otherwise have been told.

PA Support for Deployed MEUs

Because MEUs often bear the brunt of the Marine Corps' expeditionary operations that capture media attention, the need for embedded PA and combat camera support has been long recognized, and the MEU is the smallest standing combat organization to have a permanently assigned PA section.

PA sections typically consist of a PA officer, PA chief, combat correspondent, and in the case of the 22d MEU, two combat photographers and a combat videographer, although for the unit's Landing Force Sixth Fleet 1-04 (LF6F 1-04) deployment there were two videographers. While the missions of PA and combat camera are inherently different, within the MEU they are mutually supporting.

Integration into the MEU's Combat Forces

One of our overriding goals from the onset of our predeployment training program (PTP) for the LF6F 1-04 deployment was to do away with what has been called "the white van PA mindset." We strove to never have a photographer or correspondent roll up to Marines in the field, jump out of a vehicle in a clean uniform, take pictures or ask questions, and drive away.

This mentality is counterproductive in two ways. First and foremost, it reinforces the stereotype of PA Marines as garrison types unwilling to get their hands dirty, and second, it's a disservice to the PA Marine who may one day go into harm's way.

Since the MEU's ground combat element, Battalion Landing Team 1st Battalion, 6th Marines (BLT 1/6), would be main effort—or at least participate in every combat operation—our Marines were introduced early in the PTP to the battalion's companies and platoons. The PA Marines attended raid and combat skills conducted by the special operations training group and took part in every PTP exercise alongside the battalion's infantrymen.

These relationships forged early in the PTP provided untold benefits as our Marines went to the field in Afghanistan with the elements of the BLT with whom they had trained. Additionally, our constant presence during training exercises made us known qualities, not only to BLT 1/6 but also to the command element sections, Marine Medium Helicopter Squadron 266 (Reinforced), and MEU Service Support Group 22.

In addition to standard training inherent to deploying Marines (physical training, shooting courses/ranges, gas chamber, regional briefs, etc.), the PA Marines read books and articles focused on Afghan culture. For example, understanding the sensitivity of taking pictures of local women or of mosques did much to avert problems that may have arisen in the course of their coverage.

Actions on the Objective

Starting on April 24, when the MEU began pushing forces en masse out of Afghanistan's Kandahar Air Field and into the Oruzgan Province, our Marines went with them. While one Marine remained at Kandahar to facilitate logistics and cover our elements there and one stayed at Forward Operating Base (FOB) Ripley, the bulk of the section was constantly in the field.

Over the course of the next ten weeks, PA Marines participated in each named combat operation the MEU undertook, including local security operations in and around FOB Ripley. By capturing every facet of the Marines' and sailors' activities, the PA Marines' still images and video footage provide long-lasting and incontrovertible testimony of our service in south-central Afghanistan.

While the primary mission of the PA section in Afghanistan was to document for prosperity and public release the MEU's combat and civil and military operations, collateral assignments and employment included:

- Psychological operations flyers designed to engender good will between the Afghan people and coalition forces.
- Recording of arms cache discovery and destruction.
- Identification of battlefield detainees and casualties.
- Training aids for identifying and treating wounds by medical specialists.
- Support to briefers and planners.
- Treatment of wounded Taliban insurgents to dispel mistreatment allegations.
- Documentation of interrogations.
- Landing zone studies.
- Investigation of accidents and mishaps.

In addition to their primary duties, our Marines guarded detainees, helped search compounds, provided security whenever required, stood radio watch, and, when the opportunity required, engaged the enemy with direct fire.

Lessons Learned

Operating in high-intensity combat situations in some of the most difficult terrain imaginable presented its challenges, and while nothing was insurmountable, valuable lessons were learned and other practices reinforced:

- Equipment redundancy. Equipment breakdowns were overcome with redundancy. For example, $8,000 cameras were backed up with simple $200 "point-and-shoot" digital cameras.
- Resupply. The need for fresh batteries and to download images can cause an interruption of coverage unless arrangements are made prior to mission commencement. Helicopter crew chiefs on resupply missions should have been used to transfer fresh batteries and data sources instead of pulling Marines from the field and scrambling to reattach them to units in the field.

- Every Marine in the MEU who would come into contact with the media received permission classes on interview techniques and what to expect in an interview. Additionally, "smart cards" with the MEU's mission and command-approved messages and themes were distributed or available to every Marine and sailor in the MEU.
- Of course, no one is ever happy with the amount of training they go through because there is always something overlooked. Additional focus on subjects such as Pashtu phrases and key words, weapons handling, HMMWV driver school, and other such topics could have better prepared us for Afghanistan operations.

Impact of PA on the Forgotten War

After the MEU's retrograde from FOB Ripley back to Kandahar Air Field, Army Maj. Gen. Eric T. Oison, Commanding General, Combined Joint Task Force 76, addressed the 22d MEU in a mass formation. He used this opportunity to laud the MEU's service and called the unit's activities over the past ten weeks "the most successful military operation since Operation Enduring Freedom began."

The MEU's achievements in Afghanistan were truly remarkable—more than enemy fighters killed, 108 civil affairs projects begun or completed, more than 2,000 medical and dental patients treated, 2,500 weapons and 75,000 pieces of ordnance confiscated and destroyed, and nearly 60,000 Afghans registered to vote in the country's upcoming elections.

Every facet of these accomplishments was documented and in many cases released to the public via the MEU web site. Over a period of 4 months, our section released 86 news stories and more than 600 photographs to the web site and news agencies across the United States, Afghanistan, and elsewhere in the world.

During our time in Afghanistan, the American public was being assaulted almost daily with dreary and fatalistic press reporting from Iraq. Few news agencies expressed interest in covering our operations. However, when word spread, via our stories and releases, that we killed more than eighty Taliban and anticoalition militia fighters in a one-week period, reporters who had balked at embedding with us only one week earlier now clamored to join our ranks. Prior to commencing Operation Thunder Road several weeks later, we were deluged with requests from reporters seeking to cover our operations.

The news of the disruptions we caused in the Oruzgan and Zabol Provinces, where anticoalition factions had long enjoyed support, revitalized American cognizance, and therefore support, of the crucial antiterror campaign in Afghanistan.

The statement that our primary mission is to tell the story of the MEU is only partially correct. We tell the story of Marines and sailors.

After all, there is nothing more compelling than the image of a helmeted nineteen-year-old Marine dodging bullets and returning fire during a firefight with the enemies of the United States. It brings to the American public a face in which they can see their own son, wife, daughter, sister, husband, or brother, and ensures our role in the war on terror will be remembered long after our medals tarnish and ribbons fade.

---

*Published in the November 2004 *Marine Corps Gazette*. Reprinted with permission.

Appendix 6

"ASSOCIATE" IS A VERB

Hanging with the Right Crowd

By Keith Oliver*

> He that walketh with
> wise men shall be wise
>
> — Proverbs 13:20

Assuming you wear the uniform, or are otherwise associated with the U.S. Armed Forces, congratulations: you've modeled a measure of professionalism just by reading this newspaper. (And I hope, if you paid for this copy of the *Marine Corps Times* out of your own pocket, you will deduct the cost on your income tax. You rate it.)

A professional, business literature asserts, has acquired specialized training or education and stays current in his chosen field by reading, convening, and conferring with fellow professionals, often through a recognized professional association.

Think about it. Maybe you grew up in a household where Mom or Dad was a teacher, or maybe a lawyer or doctor, or a cop or firefighter. Remember those work-related magazines on the coffee table? Many were published by specific professional associations, and they were evidence that your mother or father didn't just have a job—he or she was honing a career. The publications, and perhaps the local meetings or regional or national conventions they attended, were all part of "sharpening the saw."

The profession of arms requires no less attention than civilian pursuits. In fact, given the life-and-death stakes, it requires more.

Are you a professional?

In the November 21 edition of the *Times* was published a roster of associations, a great place to start. Whether you're infantry, artillery, communications, or intelligence, there are several fine groups looking for young blood—and generously giving up sage advice and other benefits, in return.

You can't join 'em all—that's a given. But an excellent ice-breaker, and a beneficial, career-long habit to cultivate, is to at least join two: an organization dedicated to your Service, and a group designed to pursue topics peculiar to your warfighting specialty.

My senior drill instructor made it easy for us just prior to graduating Marine boot camp in 1972: we signed up for the Marine Corps Association and *Leatherneck* magazine *en masse*.

A year after leaving Parris Island, I made a lateral move into public affairs, to be met by Mustang 2nd Lt. Bob Jordan. "Fill this out," he told me. It was an application to join the U.S. Marine Corps Combat Correspondents Association, an organization which, from the perspective of my tiny, new MOS, was populated by a veritable Hall of Fame.

These were topflight civilian writers, broadcasters, and photographers specifically recruited by Headquarters Marine Corps during World War II. When the shooting stopped, these unique contributors to (and recorders of) Corps lore formed an Association "to aid the public relations and other programs of the Marine Corps."

As with other organizations, membership was expanded to include those currently on active duty. Local chapters were established Corpswide, and at the 23rd Commandant's (Gen. Wallace M. Greene, Jr.) behest, a robust awards program became the highlight of the annual national conference.

More than thirty years later, I can only look back with gratitude at the rich relationships that ensued, both personal and professional.

Later, when I eyed commissioning programs, my gunny chided me. "If you become an officer, they'll make you read the *Marine Corps Gazette*," he said. I already did. And a couple years later, I joined the U.S. Naval Institute to get *Proceedings* magazine.

Never the sharpest tool in the shed (and I've got the test scores to prove it), I first affiliated with those two organizations just to stay afloat. I wanted to keep up with the smart guys as best I could and, especially when stationed outside the mainstream, I could depend on the mailman to bring me fresh, insightful reading every month.

But what started out as necessary survival gear became a distinct advantage as my years in Marine green turned to decades.

More significant were the older, sometimes retired Marines who mentored me. I can think of a special handful who truly became surrogate uncles or fathers to me and my peers—and surrogate grandparents to my children. I received sterling family and career advice from these "Greatest Generation" reps; it went far beyond the nuts and bolts of how I might do my job better—although I got plenty of good tips in that arena, as well. To a man, I met each through some sort of military professional association.

Esprit de Corps—"Spirit of the Body"—says that we who take the oath are involved in a *team* sport. Going it alone, depending solely upon government-issue directives and, especially, failing to glean wisdom from the tribal elders of our particular trade, is near-sighted and unnecessary.

"Today's careers," states the Marine4Life website, "are built on strong personal networks." And nothing more effectively accelerates and nurtures that process than associating with others in your calling.

Join an association. It's the professional thing to do.

---

*Original manuscript prior to publication in the *Marine Corps Times,* January 23, 2006, as "Professional Organizations Help Further Careers with Advice, Personal Networks." Reprinted with permission.

Appendix 7

A WORD ABOUT BALANCE AND QUALITY OF LIFE

A Dichotomy Oversold

By Lt. Col. Keith Oliver*

> It all boils down to two things, accomplishing the
> mission and taking care of your people. And in case
> of a tie, the mission comes first.
>
> — OFFICER CANDIDATES SCHOOL INSTRUCTOR

Those words, spoken one summer many years ago at
Quantico, sounded reasonable enough to me at the
time—they still do.

August in Virginia meant the old Quonset hut classroom
at Camp Upshur was hot and sticky, so I don't remember
everything from that particular lesson the year Elvis died. I
do recall that our lecturer—staff sergeant—pointed out that,
under good leadership, the two goals were rarely in conflict. But when they were at odds, he emphasized, it was pro-
found. He used, for example, a commander having to order
his Marines to an almost certain death in battle.

In the years since, I have yet to come across a Marine
who didn't roger-up to the concept that those two bedrock
principles taught at Officer Candidates School were the right
ones; and I've never met a fellow Marine who quibbled about
their being in the correct order. Sad to say, however, the (perceived) gulf between mission accomplishment and troop wel-
fare has been deep and wide; and the "nitnoid" trivia that
has been passed off in the name of "crisis" continues to be a
growth industry.

There are those among us who don't understand that
sometimes you take your pack off, recharge the batteries, and

conduct scheduled maintenance. A disgruntled few appear to approach every project, every mission, with a mindset that suggests, "I just know there's a hard way to do this—and I'm gonna find it!"

Left unchecked, the leader who treats every tasking as the unit's top priority is inviting disaster, not only in terms of morale, but extending to family life and his own personal health.

Reality Checks

In fairness, it's easy to lose the bubble—to get so caught up in the mission that you lose sight of what's going on around you. Aviators call this lack of situational awareness "tunnel vision." And they often combat it in traditional Marine fashion, by depending on a buddy to "check six." In other words, have somebody else whom you trust look at the situation from a different perspective, compensating for your natural blind spots.

More often than not, that "somebody else" has a personal stake in your leadership style. Your wife or your noncommissioned officer in charge, for instance. For the latter, a time-tested approach is to make it crystal clear to your senior enlisted Marine upon reporting aboard that he or she has carte blanche authority and a professional responsibility to step into your office, shut the hatch, and candidly advise you of those blind spots when necessary—especially when it concerns the well-being of Marines. (Most staff noncommissioned officers require no special invitation!)

Your peers will keep you out of trouble, too, as long as you're not too proud to admit you just might not know quite everything. And a precious, probably underutilized resource in our Corps is our cadre of retired Marines—the older, the better. These tribal elders have been there/done that as warriors, parents, and grandparents. They know what's important in life in all those categories. Talk about sage advice!

Ways and Means

Make no mistake, if you decide to strike a blow for freedom, if you take up arms against the bloated spirit of workaholism, you'll be battling an entrenched enemy.

There are those who have made headway, however, and we might borrow from some of their techniques. The majority of the following examples deal with family time—a popular but scarce commodity among today's warriors. Breakfast, anyone? 30th Commandant, Gen. Carl Mundy, was said to suggest to Amphibious Warfare School classes that they give their hard-working Fleet Marine Force Marines a break once in a while by letting them eat breakfast at home with their families, reporting in at midmorning. He also cautioned aspiring company commanders against trying to make Corps history on the backs of their young Marines, running their unit into the ground during a manic, hell-bent eighteen months or so in charge.

Have you seen the islands? When Col. Wes Hammond ran the G2 shop at Fleet Marine Force Pacific in Hawaii during the height of Vietnam, he insisted that his officers take off an afternoon a week. Owing to typical Marine macho and type "A" personalities, the colonel's charges were not in full compliance. That is, until he held a social event at his quarters and, one by one, sidled up to each wife. "And tell me," he would innocently ask, "how is your husband enjoying my policy of taking an afternoon off each week? Are you getting around to see the islands?" Problem solved.

Personal salute does it. A very senior British defense official was flying into Cherry Point, to be met by the 2d Marine Aircraft Wing's commanding general (CG). When staff asked the CG, Maj. Gen. Gus Gustafson, if any sort of formal review would be required, the general assured all that his personal hand salute at planeside would suffice. "We're not Eighth and I," he said.

It's her day. One of my wife's minor military irritations (ranked just after the infamous "medical appointment phone drill") is a paper tiger called "Spouse Appreciation Day." Too many local observances consist of publishing a heartwarming message signed off by the secretary of defense, and maybe a story on the Wives' Club in the base newspaper. My SEAL commander buddy, Dave, has a better idea: he sets the watch on Spouse Appreciation Day, sending his warriors home to do Mama's bidding. It's her day, after all. How does he do that? A former boss, then commanding an operational helicopter squadron, made it a practice to give his Marines "three-day weekends" every weekend that they were in garrison. He accomplished it with imaginative scheduling and a heads-up duty section. He must have been doing something right: they captured Marine helicopter squadron of the year honors.

You asked him what? At the weekly CG's meeting at Parris Island some years ago, the Headquarters and Service Battalion commander asked the general if he'd be "granting noon Friday to noon Tuesday liberty" for the upcoming Labor Day Weekend, as had been authorized for the previous "long weekend." Then a lieutenant, I observed my seniors suck in their breath at my commanding officer's nonchalant inquiry. The CG, aware of the proven safety benefit of keeping his young Marines off the road during dangerous hours, responded, "Absolutely!"

"It's a party!" I remember as a young captain attending the final Marine Corps Birthday Ball committee meeting before our command's big event, and as we broke up, the major who was our ball chairman approached me, noting that I looked perplexed. I admitted that I was concerned that our planning didn't seem as detailed as the previous year. "Keith," he said, smiling and placing a hand on my shoulder, "it's a party!"

Talk is cheap. Striking a balance between the demands of "Mother Corps" and "quality of life" is no responsibility for the weak of heart. It's one thing to state a policy of healthy balance; it's quite another to live it, to lead it, when we're in the thick of the maelstrom.

U.S. Army Col. Bob Caslen, an airborne brigade commander, set the bar high in his November 1998 *Command* article:

> Our men and women are searching for examples of uncompromising ethical and moral standards, and assessing whether this military way of life is worth . . . their and their family's (commitment).
>
> They're watching how we handle stress, pressure, failures and successes. And they're watching how we balance our professional commitments, family needs, community involvement, and our own personal spiritual lives.

The colonel's right. We may "look good on paper" and acquire all the right "ticket punches" but, all the while, might our subordinates be using a measuring stick that we have yet to fully appreciate? After all, theirs is the measurement that really counts, isn't it?

---

*Published in the June 1999 *Marine Corps Gazette*. Reprinted with permission.

INDEX

ABOUT THE AUTHOR

Keith Oliver has spent more than thirty years telling the Marine Corps story, first as an enlisted combat correspondent and later as a public affairs officer during real-world operations in Lebanon, Panama, and Somalia, in addition to deploying to Operations Desert Storm and Iraqi Freedom.

Practicing what he preaches, this Eagle Scout has been heavily involved in base and community issues throughout his career, including active service in Scouting, Royal Rangers, Kiwanis, and Civitan. The Havelock, North Carolina, Chamber of Commerce named Keith "Member of the Year" in 1991.

A sports editor for his hometown (Eustis, Florida) newspaper at age eighteen, Oliver's aggressive, outside-the-box approach has garnered numerous awards for him and his public affairs shops around the Corps. The former U.S. Naval Academy English instructor retired as a colonel in 2004 and today chairs the Public Affairs Leadership Department at the Fort Meade, Maryland-based Defense Information School. Keith also has served as national president of the U.S. Marine Corps Combat Correspondents Association.

The Asbury College (Wilmore, Kentucky) alum has a Master of Arts in communication from the University of Oklahoma as well as graduate degrees from the Naval War College and the Industrial College of the Armed Forces, where he also completed the Information Strategies Program.

The Naval Institute Press is the book-publishing arm of the U.S. Naval Institute, a private, nonprofit, membership society for sea service professionals and others who share an interest in naval and maritime affairs. Established in 1873 at the U.S. Naval Academy in Annapolis, Maryland, where its offices remain today, the Naval Institute has members worldwide.

Members of the Naval Institute support the education programs of the society and receive the influential monthly magazine *Proceedings* or the colorful bimonthly magazine *Naval History* and discounts on fine nautical prints and on ship and aircraft photos. They also have access to the transcripts of the Institute's Oral History Program and get discounted admission to any of the Institute-sponsored seminars offered around the country.

The Naval Institute's book-publishing program, begun in 1898 with basic guides to naval practices, has broadened its scope to include books of more general interest. Now the Naval Institute Press publishes about seventy titles each year, ranging from how-to books on boating and navigation to battle histories, biographies, ship and aircraft guides, and novels. Institute members receive significant discounts on the Press's more than eight hundred books in print.

Full-time students are eligible for special half-price membership rates. Life memberships are also available.

For a free catalog describing Naval Institute Press books currently available, and for further information about joining the U.S. Naval Institute, please write to:

Member Services
U.S. Naval Institute
291 Wood Road
Annapolis, MD 21402-5034
Telephone: (800) 233-8764
Fax: (410) 571-1703
Web address: www.usni.org